The Complete

MEDITERRANEAN

DIET COOKBOOK

FOR BEGINNERS

Your Guide to Effortless Healthy Eating: 56-Day Meal Plan and Recipes Included, with Weekly Shopping Lists

Vita Nourish

CONTENTS

INTRODUCTION — 3

BREAKFAST RECIPES — 11

SALAD RECIPES — 20

FISH AND SEAFOOD RECIPES — 30

POULTRY AND MEAT RECIPES — 40

VEGETABLE RECIPES — 51

SNACK RECIPES — 60

DESSERT RECIPES — 65

56-DAY MEAL PLAN — 69

COOKING CONVERSION CHART — 73

SHOPPING LISTS — 74

INDEX — 79

CONCLUSION — 80

FREE BONUS — 81

Introduction

Picture this: a table laid out with a colorful array of fresh fruits, crisp vegetables, a platter of freshly caught fish drizzled in golden olive oil, bread that crackles when you break it, and a bottle of good red wine. This is more than just a meal; it's a lifestyle. Welcome to the Mediterranean diet, a culinary journey that traces the eating habits of Greece and Southern Italy, a diet so simple yet profoundly beneficial.

The Mediterranean diet is more than just food on a plate. It's a way of life, a route to living not just longer, but healthier and happier. Imagine, not just looking good but feeling good, with a sharper mind, stronger heart, and even a defense system against life's more serious ailments, such as strokes and cancer.

Science doesn't lie. Renowned institutions like Harvard University have thrown their weight behind the Mediterranean diet. Their research suggests that following this diet can reduce the risk of heart disease and cancer by an impressive 65 percent and lower the likelihood of diabetes by half. On top of this, it keeps you trim and fit, steering clear of unwanted weight gain.

These benefits are just the tip of the iceberg. Countless other studies sing the praises of the Mediterranean diet, attributing it to a healthier and happier life. So it's no wonder that thousands of Americans are joining the bandwagon, basking in its wholesome glow. It's an eating plan that keeps your brain sharp, fights off depression, and promotes a robust cardiovascular system. Did we mention it's delicious too?

At this point, you might be thinking, "This all sounds great, but diets are tough to stick to." The beauty of the Mediterranean diet lies in its ability to satiate your hunger more effectively than any low-carb or no-carb diet. Rich in fiber, it ensures your heart and digestive health are in perfect condition, keeping your weight gain in check.

But what makes up the Mediterranean diet? It's a harmonious blend of whole, unprocessed foods brimming with vitamins, minerals, and antioxidants. Fruits and vegetables, whole grains, healthy fats, fish and seafood, herbs and spices, lean meats, dairy products, and the occasional glass of red wine. These food groups, when part of our everyday meal plan, open the door to a multitude of health benefits, including a healthier heart, reduced risk of chronic diseases, and overall better quality of life.

Ready to give it a shot? This Mediterranean diet cookbook is your passport to this extraordinary lifestyle. We have curated delicious, easy-to-prepare recipes that allow you to relish in the Mediterranean diet's benefits without a hiccup. We provide meals for every day of the week, enabling you to tailor your diet to your taste buds' content. What's more, each recipe comes with nutritional information to help you make healthier food choices.

The world's health statistics may seem grim. Over half of the population worldwide is projected to be overweight or obese by 2040. But you have the power to change your story, and the Mediterranean diet could be your lifesaver. It's time to take a proactive stand for your health and the health of your loved ones. Embrace the Mediterranean lifestyle and let it do wonders for your body. Get ready to embark on this culinary adventure and remember, it's not just a diet, it's a way of life.

What is the Mediterranean Diet?

What, you might ask, is all the fuss about this Mediterranean diet? Well, pull up a chair, grab a fresh, crisp apple, and let's delve into this culinary journey together. You see, unlike those conventional diets that corner you into calorie-counting or banning certain food groups, the Mediterranean diet stands in stark contrast. It's more about adopting a healthier lifestyle with a diverse palette of foods. It invites you to indulge in an abundance of vibrant fruits and veggies, heart-healthy whole grains, protein-packed legumes and nuts, scrumptious seafood, and the show-stealer, olive oil. You also get to enjoy cheese, yogurt, and wine, but just like a great movie cameo, they're best in small, memorable appearances. And let's not forget that occasional guest star - red meat.

The beauty of this diet? It revolves around minimally processed foods, delivering a flavorful fiesta of nutrition in every bite. A little imagination can transform these ingredients into a masterpiece on your plate. So, sharpen those culinary skills and find joy in discovering tantalizing combinations that hit the spot for you.

But don't be mistaken - the Mediterranean diet isn't just about the food. No siree! It also endorses physical activity (choose what tickles your fancy), and that ever-important social connection. Basking in the company of loved ones over a meal or exchanging laughs can do wonders for your mood. You see, it's not just a diet; it's a way of life, emphasizing quality over quantity, savoring each morsel, and cultivating a healthier, happier you.

This bountiful diet doesn't just promise a tantalizing taste adventure; it delivers a ticket to a life rich in health and devoid of disease. And, it's not rigid. You can tailor it to your preferences and lifestyle, weaving in elements like regular exercise and good quality sleep.

The Mediterranean diet is your ally for weight loss, turbocharging your body's fat-burning potential. It's a natural weight management program that won't have you pulling your hair out. Beyond the scale, it helps you live a fuller life, shielding you from health foes like heart disease, diabetes, and cancer, thanks to its wholesome, antioxidant-rich foods.

And guess what? This diet isn't just an adult's game; it's kid-friendly, too. In an age where many kids fall prey to obesity due to a lack of fruits and veggies and a love for junk food, this diet shines as a beacon of hope. It equips them with the right balance of nutrients, ensuring they grow strong, healthy, and emotionally stable. The result? Better academic performance and enhanced social skills.

So, if you're a parent eager for your child to lead a healthy, robust life, this diet style fits the bill. It's a priceless lesson in healthy eating habits from a tender age. Plus, it helps stave off health risks like diabetes, heart disease, and cancer, all while supercharging their brain power.

To top it all off, the Mediterranean diet keeps you satiated longer than other diets, helping keep mood swings in check and stress at bay. Whether you're prepping for a job interview or a stressful exam, this diet has your back. And the best part? It can set you on the path to steady, sustainable weight loss without the headache of calorie counting or complex recipes.

So, ready to make every meal a Mediterranean feast and embrace a lifestyle that offers health, happiness, and a side of deliciousness? Buckle up, because this journey is one you're going to relish.

Health Benefits of the Mediterranean Diet

Do you know, my dear friends, how the Mediterranean diet can transform your life? Settle in and sip a cup of green tea, as I unfold this fairytale world of healthy eating.

Let's start with the most important - your health. According to numerous scientific studies, the Mediterranean diet helps control blood sugar levels and combats cardiovascular diseases, two cunning diseases of our time. Instead of just taking medicine, why not wield the culinary sword and engage in the battle yourself?

All this is possible thanks to a diet rich in magical vegetables, fruits, and grains, and scarce in fatty meat and industrially processed products. No fast food, no half products - just pure, natural food that originates from Mother Nature.

Weight loss? That's just a nice bonus! The Mediterranean diet doesn't require you to calculate each calorie, instead, it teaches you to enjoy the taste of fresh produce and respect your body.

Yes, this may sound like a dream, but it is nothing more than the result of how we care for ourselves. If we want to live a long and healthy life, why not start with what we eat?

The Mediterranean diet has made waves across the medical community due to its heart-hugging properties. But that's just the tip of the iceberg. This culinary lifestyle hides a trove of wellness treasures that extend beyond the cardiovascular realm. Let's dive deeper into this elixir of longevity:

For Heart Health and Stroke Shielding

Our diet is the master puppeteer behind our heart's well-being. It juggles our good cholesterol, blood sugar, blood pressure, and weight, aiming for a harmonious balance. Picture the food you ingest as messengers, carrying news to each of these players.

Many of those in danger's way are counseled to embrace a low-fat diet, a crusade against all fats, from the slick oils to the unassuming nuts and the scarlet culprit, red meat.

Why so? Because the Mediterranean diet, a cauldron of unsaturated fats, suppresses the villains of bad cholesterol while cheering for the heroes of good cholesterol. To understand this, imagine cholesterol as a waxy warrior belonging to the steroid clan of the molecular kingdom. It's an essential brick in the cell wall and a stepping-stone to fat-soluble vitamins, such as Vitamin D.

There are two main knights in the cholesterol realm - HDL (high-density lipoproteins) and LDL (low-density lipoproteins). They are transport vessels for cholesterol particles, made of protein and fats. LDLs embark on a journey from the liver to the body's cells, while HDLs mop up any stray cholesterol from the tissues and return it to the liver for reprocessing. Therefore, HDLs are hailed as the "good guys", sweeping away any cholesterol loitering in the bloodstream before it sticks to the arteries. LDL, on the other hand, is dubbed the "bad guy". An overload of cholesterol in the bloodstream could spike the risk of heart disease, especially atherosclerosis. That's why the equilibrium between HDL and LDL is a matter of life and death.

Spotlight on Trans-Fats

Trans-fats masquerade as hydrogenated or partially hydrogenated oils. They could be soy, canola, or any partly hydrogenated "vegetable" oil. This is the nutritional grim reaper, the worst form of fat you can invite into your body.

The Mayo Clinic has flagged trans-fats as saboteurs that boost LDL levels while deflating HDL levels. This synthetic villain lurks in processed goods and other packaged foods. Apart from disturbing the HDL/LDL harmony, it elevates blood triglycerides and encourages plaque build-up on arterial walls.

A star on the Mediterranean diet stage is fatty fish - a choir of lake trout, salmon, sardines, herring, mackerel, and whitefish, abundant in omega-3 fatty acids. This nutrient pacifies blood clotting and lowers triglyceride levels. High triglyceride levels can spell a heart disease curse. Omega-3 fatty acids also contribute to blood pressure regulation, reducing the risk of sudden heart attacks, and bolstering the health of our blood vessels.

Keynotes of a Mediterranean Diet:

- Olive oil: the cornerstone of fat in this diet.
- A glass of red wine often graces the dining table.
- A vibrant parade of vegetables and seasonal fresh fruits at every meal.
- Whole grain pasta and bread join the feast without any second thoughts.
- Meat portions are controlled and red meat is a rare guest.
- The flavor palette sings with garlic, basil, oregano, lemon, rosemary, and mint.

The Mediterranean diet underscores the importance of daily activity, stress unwinding, and cherishing moments with loved ones. By enriching your menu with plant-based foods and injecting regular daily activities, you're not just kindling your heart health, but the flame of overall well-being.

Age-Related Muscle and Bone Weakness

The relentless hands of time often rob us of muscle mass and bone density, leaving us vulnerable. However, like an ancient philosopher's stone, the Mediterranean diet could hold the secret to preserving our strength and vitality even as we age. Filled with the likes of fish, nuts, and legumes, this eating style provides a steady stream of protein. This is the elixir of youth that our body uses to build and repair tissues, maintaining our muscle mass against the sands of time.

Alzheimer's and Parkinson's Disease

The Mediterranean diet isn't just a guardian of the heart, but also a protector of the mind. It acts as a strong fortress, shielding against the shadowy specters of Alzheimer's and Parkinson's. Fruits, vegetables, olive oil, and wine, these keys of the Mediterranean diet, open doors to a healthy brain. They act like an army of antioxidants, driving away the marauding oxidative stress that causes the mental fog and memory loss associated with these diseases.

Type 2 Diabetes

As we've already seen, the Mediterranean diet is a master of balance. This harmony extends to our blood sugar levels, which can often resemble a wild, untamed beast. In the grand theatre of our body, insulin is the ringmaster, keeping the glucose beast in check. But in those with Type 2 Diabetes, this master of control is either absent or ignored. The Mediterranean diet, rich in fiber and healthy fats, helps by slowing down digestion. This delays the entrance of glucose into our bloodstream, giving insulin a fighting chance to keep things under control. As a result, blood sugar spikes are tamed and Type 2 Diabetes is kept at bay.

Cancer

Last, but definitely not least, the Mediterranean diet wields a powerful weapon against the terrifying titan known as Cancer. The fruits, vegetables, and whole grains in this diet form a triumvirate of health, bursting with antioxidants. These mighty warriors wage war on harmful free radicals, preventing them from damaging our cells and triggering the deadly mutations that can lead to cancer.

In summary, the Mediterranean diet is not just a culinary tradition. It is a symphony of nutrients, a festival of flavors, and a bastion of health. It is a guardian of our hearts and minds, a protector against the ravages of age, a ringmaster of balance, and a warrior against disease. So, take a seat at this lavish feast and savor the vibrant, life-affirming bounty of the Mediterranean.

How to Follow the Mediterranean Diet?

Eat a Rainbow: The secret of the Mediterranean diet is not buried treasure, it's openly displayed in nature's palette. Fill your plate with colorful fruits and vegetables; let it reflect the golden sunrises, emerald fields, and ruby sunsets of the Mediterranean. Each color is a banner of different nutrients, and together they form a vibrant mosaic of health.

Go Whole or Go Home: In the land of the Mediterranean, white flour is as rare as a white peacock. Whole grains are the humble heroes here, the unsung warriors who fight against heart disease and diabetes. So, set aside your bleached bread and polished rice, and welcome the hearty embrace of whole wheat, bulgur, oats, and quinoa.

Rethink your Protein: The Mediterranean Sea is not just a body of water, it's a cradle of life. Its depths teem with fish rich in omega-3 fatty acids, the guardians of heart health. Occasionally, you might feast on poultry, and even less often, on red meat, which is consumed as sparingly as a rare vintage wine.

Embrace Healthy Fats: Fear not the olive! In the Mediterranean, olives are more than just food - they are a gift from the gods, a source of life-giving oil. It's time to wave goodbye to the hydrogenated oils and trans fats of the West and open your heart to the monounsaturated fat of olives.

Spice it Up: The Mediterranean diet does not imprison you in a bland culinary cage. Quite the opposite! Its symphony of flavors sings in every bite. Herbs and spices are the maestros of this orchestra, conducting a composition of taste and health. So, embrace the exotic dance of garlic, the warm hug of cinnamon, and the vibrant personality of oregano.

Practice Portion Control: The Mediterranean lifestyle does not endorse gluttony. It teaches you to enjoy your meal, to savor each bite, and to be content with smaller portions. Imagine your meal as a painting - you want it to be pleasing to the eye, but not overwhelming.

Drink in Moderation: The Mediterranean tradition doesn't forbid alcohol, but it encourages you to consume it in moderation. Wine, especially red wine, is treated with respect and is often part of meals, enjoyed in good company. Remember, though, that every coin has two sides - the same wine that can benefit your heart in moderation can wreak havoc when consumed excessively.

Engage in Physical Activity: The Mediterranean lifestyle is not just about food. It's about living with zest and vitality, about celebrating the human body through movement. So, dance like the Greeks, hike like the Spaniards, swim like the Italians, and cherish the joy of physical activity.

Embarking on a Mediterranean diet is less about strict adherence to a regimented diet plan and more about embracing a holistic, joyous lifestyle. It's about living in harmony with nature, rejoicing in its bounty, and respecting your body's needs. As you sail on this journey, remember, the wind might not always be in your favor, but adjusting your sails can always get you to your destination.

What Foods Does the Mediterranean Diet Consist Of?

Allow me to guide you through the labyrinth of the Mediterranean pantry, a treasure trove of foods that taste as splendid as they are beneficial to our health. Each ingredient, like a character in a grand opus, plays its part in a symphony of nutrition and flavor. Together, they weave a rich tapestry of wellness, the threads of which span from the azure coasts of the Mediterranean to your very dining table.

Fruits and Vegetables: Nature's jewel box holds a plethora of precious gems. Each bite of these vibrant foods, packed with antioxidants and fiber, battles the rogue elements within your body, the free radicals, guarding you against chronic diseases and aging.

Whole Grains: The faithful guardians of your health, whole grains, slow to release their energy, maintain your blood sugar levels, preventing the highs and lows of the blood sugar roller coaster. Rich in fiber, they support digestion and contribute to satiety, playing a vital role in weight management.

Healthy Fats: The lifeblood of the Mediterranean diet, olive oil, along with avocados, nuts, and seeds, delivers heart-healthy monounsaturated fats. This golden elixir helps lower bad cholesterol levels, while the crunchy cadre of nuts and seeds provides essential vitamins and minerals.

Fish and Seafood: The siren song of the sea draws you in with an array of seafood rich in omega-3 fatty acids. These beneficial fats protect your heart like a steadfast sailor, keeping the treacherous waves of heart disease at bay.

Poultry, Eggs, and Dairy: These actors provide a protein-packed performance, supporting muscle health, while also delivering a hit of B vitamins and calcium. In moderation, they lend their nutritional prowess without stealing the spotlight.

Red Wine: This crimson poet whispers verses of resveratrol and antioxidants that help protect the heart. But remember, overindulgence can drown the verse in a sea of health problems. So, savor the wine's wisdom with caution.

Herbs and Spices: The maestros of the Mediterranean symphony, herbs, and spices bring not just flavor, but a cascade of health benefits. They are potent antioxidants, anti-inflammatories, and boosters of heart health, lending their magic to every dish they grace.

Red and Processed Meats: These infrequent guests, while adding depth of flavor, also come with a health caution. High in saturated fats, they should be consumed in moderation to maintain the balance of this rich, healthful diet.

Feast on the Mediterranean diet, a culinary journey that satiates the palate and nurtures the body. Its vibrant dance of flavors and nutritional abundance is a love letter to life itself, an invitation to savor the richness of health and the joy of great taste in every bite.

Cooking Techniques and Tools for Recipes

Venturing into the sun-dappled realm of the Mediterranean kitchen is an adventure akin to exploring an old-world marketplace, bursting with color, aroma, and a sense of timeless tradition. The Mediterranean culinary journey is less about following a rigid set of rules, and more about embracing the artistry of cooking. We shall immerse in the techniques, not just as a set of instructions, but as harmonious melodies serenading fresh produce into dishes that echo with the Mediterranean soul.

Techniques:

1. **Embracing Olive Oil's Liquid Gold**: Just as a maestro conducts an orchestra, olive oil leads the ensemble of Mediterranean flavors. Use it lavishly for sautéing, roasting, and dressing. Its emerald essence dances with the ingredients, lending a silky texture and an earthy depth of flavor.

2. **Grilling - An Open-Air Ballet**: In the Mediterranean, grilling is not just a cooking technique, but a celebration of the outdoors. Vegetables, fish, and lean meats waltz on the grill, their flavors intensifying under the heat, emerging with smoky notes and a caramelized sweetness that teases the senses.

3. **Slow Cooking - An Ode to Patience**: The Mediterranean style respects the art of slow cooking, where flavors are given time to develop and mingle, creating a culinary tapestry that tells a tale of patience and passion.

4. **Fresh Herbs - Nature's Confetti**: Toss them into salads, simmer them in sauces, or use them as a garnish. Fresh herbs are like festive confetti sprinkled across the Mediterranean dishes, imparting an aromatic essence and vibrant color that is truly a feast for the senses.

Tools:

1. **Mortar and Pestle - The Time-Honored Duo**: To grind spices or make traditional pastes like pesto, the mortar, and pestle are your trusty companions. They preserve the natural oils of ingredients, helping release their fullest potential in your dishes.

2. **Quality Knives - The Artisan's Brush**: Just as a painter needs a brush, a cook needs quality knives. From finely chopping herbs to dicing fresh vegetables, they ensure precision and ease in the kitchen.

3. **Cast-Iron Grills and Skillets - The Sturdy Dance Floor**: Perfect for grilling and sautéing the Mediterranean way, their excellent heat retention makes for even cooking, while their sturdiness stands the test of time, much like the Mediterranean diet itself.

4. **Dutch Oven - The Mighty Cauldron**: Ideal for slow cooking, a Dutch oven allows heat to surround the food uniformly, gently coaxing the flavors to blossom over time.

The Mediterranean kitchen is a symphony of timeless techniques and tools, a delicate dance of traditions that invite you to savor each moment of the cooking process. It implores you to engage with your ingredients, to coax out their flavors, and to create meals that aren't just nourishing for the body, but also the soul. With every stir, slice, and sizzle, you're not just preparing a meal; you're crafting an edible piece of Mediterranean art.

How to Use This Book

Recipes: Embark on a flavorful journey with each recipe! Every step is a stroll through the Mediterranean streets - you will find preparation time, cooking time, total time, and servings clearly marked. If a recipe calls for extra marinating or waiting, it's noted specially. Vivid, colorful images accompany each recipe, along with a detailed list of ingredients and step-by-step cooking instructions. Nutrition facts and required equipment are your trusty companions on this culinary expedition.

Meal Plan: Navigate your diet like a seasoned sailor using our detailed meal plans. They're your charts to a world of breakfasts, lunches, dinners, desserts, and snacks. For seamless exploration, page numbers for each recipe are conveniently provided. Plus, the daily calorie count is featured in a separate column, helping you steer your health journey confidently.

Weekly Shopping Lists: Consider these your treasure maps to nutritional gold. Listed are the items and quantities needed to create the sumptuous dishes for the corresponding week in the meal plan.

Index: Your alphabetized compass to all the recipes in this book, complete with page numbers. It's your quick reference to set sail to the next delicious destination.

Cooking Conversion Chart: Here, you will find your navigator's tools: 'Dry Volume Equivalents', 'Liquid Volume Equivalents', 'Temperature Equivalents', and 'Weight Equivalents'. These charts are your trusty guides to conquering the culinary seas without getting lost in translation.

A Final Note:

May this book be your lighthouse, guiding you through the rich and vibrant waters of Mediterranean cooking. As you turn each page, may you be embraced by the warm sun, kissed by the sea breeze, and nourished by the earth of this enchanting region. Bon Voyage and Bon Appétit!

BREAKFAST RECIPES

Classic Greek Yogurt Parfait

Prep time: 10 min **Total time:** 10 min
Cook time: 0 min **Servings:** 2

Ingredients:

- 2 cups Greek yogurt
- 1/2 cup granola
- 1 cup mixed berries (strawberries, blueberries, raspberries)
- 4 tablespoon honey
- 1 teaspoon vanilla extract
- Fresh mint leaves for garnish (optional)

Directions:

1. In a serving glass or bowl, layer half of the Greek yogurt.
2. Sprinkle half of the granola over the yogurt layer.
3. Add half of the mixed berries on top of the granola.
4. Drizzle half of the honey over the berries.
5. Repeat the layers with the remaining yogurt, granola, berries, and honey.
6. Finish with a drizzle of vanilla extract on top.
7. Garnish with fresh mint leaves if desired.
8. Serve immediately and enjoy this refreshing and nutritious Classic Greek Yogurt Parfait.

Nutrition: Calories: 290; Fat: 3g; Carbs: 40g; Protein: 24g; Sugar: 30g; Fiber: 3g

Equipment: None.

Scrambled Eggs with Spinach and Feta

Prep time: 10 min **Total time:** 18 min
Cook time: 8 min **Servings:** 2

Ingredients:

- 4 large eggs
- 1/4 cup milk
- Salt and pepper to taste
- 1 tablespoon olive oil
- 2 cups fresh spinach, chopped
- 1/4 cup feta cheese, crumbled

Directions:

1. In a bowl, whisk the eggs, milk, salt, and pepper.
2. Heat olive oil in a skillet over medium heat.

3. Add spinach to the skillet and sauté until wilted.
4. Pour the egg mixture over the spinach and cook, stirring constantly until eggs are set.
5. Sprinkle with feta cheese, and continue to cook for another minute.
6. Serve hot and enjoy your flavorful Scrambled Eggs with Spinach and Feta.

Nutrition: Calories: 280; Fat: 20g; Carbs: 5g; Protein: 20g; Sugar: 4g; Fiber: 1g

Equipment: Non-stick skillet.

Avocado and Tomato Whole Grain Toast

Prep time: 10 min **Total time:** 15 min
Cook time: 5 min   **Servings:** 2

Ingredients:

- 2 slices whole grain bread
- 1 ripe avocado
- 1 medium tomato
- 1 tablespoon olive oil
- Salt and pepper to taste
- 1/2 teaspoon red chili flakes (optional)
- Fresh basil leaves for garnish

Directions:

1. Toast the whole grain bread to your desired level of crispiness.
2. Cut the avocado in half, remove the pit, and scoop the flesh into a bowl. Mash it with a fork and season with salt and pepper.
3. Slice the tomato thinly.
4. Spread the mashed avocado evenly over the toasted bread.
5. Layer the tomato slices on top of the avocado.
6. Drizzle with olive oil and sprinkle with red chili flakes if using.
7. Garnish with fresh basil leaves.
8. Serve immediately and enjoy the delightful combination of creamy avocado and juicy tomato on crunchy whole grain toast.

Nutrition: Calories: 310; Fat: 20g; Carbs: 27g; Protein: 6g; Sugar: 3g; Fiber: 9g

Equipment: Toaster.

Mediterranean Omelet with Olives and Tomatoes

Prep time: 10 min **Total time:** 17 min
Cook time: 7 min   **Servings:** 2

Ingredients:

- 4 large eggs
- 1/4 cup milk
- Salt and pepper to taste
- 1 tablespoon olive oil
- 1/2 cup cherry tomatoes, halved

- ✓ 1/4 cup olives, pitted and sliced
- ✓ 1/4 cup feta cheese, crumbled
- ✓ 2 tablespoons fresh parsley, chopped

Directions:

1. In a bowl, whisk together the eggs, milk, salt, and pepper.
2. Heat the olive oil in a non-stick skillet over medium heat.
3. Pour the egg mixture into the skillet and cook for a few minutes until the edges begin to set.
4. Add the cherry tomatoes, olives, and feta cheese over the top of the eggs.
5. Continue to cook until the omelet is set but still slightly soft in the center.
6. Fold the omelet in half and cook for another minute until fully set.
7. Sprinkle with fresh parsley and serve immediately.

Nutrition: Calories: 280; Fat: 20g; Carbs: 5g; Protein: 18g; Sugar: 3g; Fiber: 1g

Equipment: Non-stick skillet.

Chia Seed Pudding with Fresh Berries

Prep time: 15 min **Total time:** 4h 15 min
Chill time: 4 hours **Servings:** 2

Ingredients:

- ✓ 1/4 cup chia seeds
- ✓ 1 cup almond milk (unsweetened)
- ✓ 1 tablespoon honey or maple syrup
- ✓ 1/2 teaspoon vanilla extract
- ✓ 1/2 cup fresh berries (strawberries, blueberries, raspberries, etc.)
- ✓ A pinch of salt

Directions:

1. In a medium-sized bowl, whisk together the chia seeds, almond milk, honey or maple syrup, vanilla extract, and a pinch of salt.
2. Cover the bowl and refrigerate for at least 4 hours, or overnight, until the mixture thickens to a pudding-like consistency.
3. Divide the pudding into two serving glasses or bowls.
4. Top with fresh berries and a drizzle of honey or maple syrup, if desired.
5. Serve chilled, and enjoy your nutritious and delightful Chia Seed Pudding with Fresh Berries.

Nutrition: Calories: 210; Fat: 9g; Carbs: 26g; Protein: 5g; Sugar: 11g; Fiber: 12g

Equipment: Medium-sized bowl; Whisk; Serving glasses or bowls.

Whole Grain Pancakes with Fig Compote

Prep time: 20 min **Total time:** 35 min
Cook time: 15 min **Servings:** 4

Ingredients:

- ✓ 1 cup whole grain flour
- ✓ 1 tablespoon sugar
- ✓ 1 teaspoon baking powder
- ✓ 1/2 teaspoon baking soda
- ✓ 1/2 teaspoon salt
- ✓ 1 cup buttermilk
- ✓ 1 large egg
- ✓ 2 tablespoons unsalted butter, melted
- ✓ 1 teaspoon vanilla extract
  For the Fig Compote:

- ✓ 1 cup fresh or dried figs, chopped
- ✓ 1/2 cup water
- ✓ 1/4 cup honey
- ✓ 1/2 teaspoon cinnamon

Directions:

1. In a large bowl, combine the flour, sugar, baking powder, baking soda, and salt.
2. In another bowl, whisk together the buttermilk, egg, melted butter, and vanilla extract. Add to the dry ingredients and stir until just combined.
3. Heat a skillet over medium heat and lightly grease. Pour 1/4 cup of batter for each pancake and cook until bubbles form on top, then flip and cook until golden brown.
4. For the Fig Compote, combine the figs, water, honey, and cinnamon in a small saucepan. Simmer over low heat for 10-15 minutes until thickened.
5. Serve pancakes topped with the Fig Compote and enjoy your delicious Whole Grain Pancakes with Fig Compote.

Nutrition: Calories: 320; Fat: 8g; Carbs: 56g; Protein: 9g; Sugar: 26g; Fiber: 7g

Equipment: Large bowl; Skillet; Small saucepan.

Veggie Frittata with Herbs

Prep time: 15 min   **Total time:** 40 min
Cook time: 25 min   **Servings:** 2

Ingredients:

- ✓ 6 large eggs
- ✓ 1/4 cup milk
- ✓ Salt and pepper to taste
- ✓ 1 tablespoon olive oil
- ✓ 1/2 cup bell peppers, diced (red and yellow for color)
- ✓ 1/4 cup red onion, finely chopped
- ✓ 1/4 cup zucchini, diced
- ✓ 1/4 cup cherry tomatoes, halved
- ✓ 1/4 cup feta cheese, crumbled (optional)
- ✓ 2 tablespoons fresh herbs (parsley, chives, and basil), finely chopped

Directions:

1. In a medium mixing bowl, whisk together eggs, milk, salt, and pepper until well combined. Set aside.
2. Heat olive oil in an oven-safe skillet over medium heat. Add the bell peppers, red onion, and zucchini. Sauté for about 5 minutes, or until vegetables are slightly softened.
3. Add cherry tomatoes to the skillet and cook for an additional 2 minutes.

4. Pour the egg mixture over the vegetables in the skillet, ensuring even distribution.
5. Sprinkle the crumbled feta cheese (if using) and herbs on top.
6. Allow the frittata to cook without stirring for about 4-5 minutes, or until the edges start to set.
7. Preheat the oven broiler. Transfer the skillet to the oven and broil for 3-5 minutes, or until the top is set and slightly golden.
8. Remove from the oven and let it sit for a couple of minutes before slicing.

Nutrition: Calories: 320; Fat: 22g; Carbs: 12g; Protein: 18g; Sugar: 5g; Fiber: 3g

Equipment: Oven-safe skillet; Medium mixing bowl; Whisk.

Mediterranean Breakfast Salad with Prosciutto and Figs

Prep time: 10 min **Total time:** 10 min
Cook time: 0 min **Servings:** 2

Ingredients:

- 4 slices of prosciutto, thinly sliced
- 4 fresh figs, quartered
- 2 cups mixed greens (like arugula, spinach, and frisée)
- 1/4 cup feta cheese, crumbled
- 8 cherry tomatoes, halved
- 1/4 cup kalamata olives, pitted and halved
- 2 tablespoons extra-virgin olive oil
- 1 tablespoon balsamic vinegar
- Salt and pepper, to taste
- 1 tablespoon fresh basil, chopped
- 1 tablespoon fresh mint, chopped

Directions:

1. In a large bowl, combine the mixed greens, cherry tomatoes, and olives.
2. Drizzle with olive oil and balsamic vinegar. Toss to coat the greens evenly.
3. Season with salt and pepper, then sprinkle with basil and mint.
4. Divide the salad among two serving plates.
5. Arrange two slices of prosciutto on each plate.
6. Place the quartered figs evenly among the plates.
7. Sprinkle crumbled feta cheese over the salads.
8. Serve immediately, ideally with a slice of toasted whole grain bread if desired.

Nutrition: Calories: 320; Fat: 18g; Carbs: 27g; Protein: 10g; Sugar: 16g; Fiber: 4g

Equipment: Salad bowl; Salad server or tongs; Knife; Chopping board.

Almond Granola Parfait with Apricots

Prep time: 10 min **Total time:** 10 min
Cook time: 0 min **Servings:** 2

Ingredients:

- Greek yogurt: 1 cup
- Almond granola: 1/2 cup
- Fresh apricots, sliced: 4
- Honey: 2 tablespoons
- Almonds, slivered: 1 tablespoon
- Mint leaves (for garnish): 2-3

Directions:

1. In a serving glass or bowl, layer a quarter of the Greek yogurt at the bottom.
2. Add a quarter of the almond granola over the yogurt.
3. Place a few slices of fresh apricots over the granola.
4. Drizzle with a tablespoon of honey.
5. Repeat the layers with the remaining yogurt, granola, apricots, and honey.
6. Top with slivered almonds.
7. Garnish with mint leaves.
8. Serve immediately and enjoy.

Nutrition: Calories: 280; Fat: 7g; Carbs: 40g; Protein: 12g; Sugar: 25g; Fiber: 4g

Equipment: Serving glasses or bowls.

Poached Eggs over Olive and Herb Focaccia

Prep time: 10 min   **Total time:** 15 min
Cook time: 5 min   **Servings:** 2

Ingredients:

- Eggs: 4 large
- Olive and herb focaccia: 2 slices
- White vinegar: 1 tablespoon
- Salt and pepper: to taste
- Olive oil: 1 tablespoon
- Fresh parsley, chopped: for garnish

Directions:

1. Fill a deep skillet or pot with about 3 inches of water. Bring the water to a gentle simmer, then add white vinegar.
2. Crack each egg into a small bowl. Gently slide the egg from the bowl into the simmering water, one at a time.
3. Poach the eggs for about 3-4 minutes for a runny yolk, or longer if you prefer a firmer yolk.
4. While eggs are poaching, toast the olive and herb focaccia slices until they are golden brown.
5. Using a slotted spoon, carefully remove each poached egg from the water and drain on a paper towel.
6. Place each toasted focaccia on a plate, then top with two poached eggs.
7. Drizzle with olive oil and season with salt and pepper.
8. Garnish with chopped parsley and serve immediately.

Nutrition: Calories: 350; Fat: 14g; Carbs: 38g; Protein: 14g; Sugar: 2g; Fiber: 2g

Equipment: Deep skillet or pot; Slotted spoon; Toaster or oven.

Shakshuka with Bell Peppers and Tomatoes

Prep time: 10 min　　**Total time:** 30 min
Cook time: 20 min　　**Servings:** 2

Ingredients:

- ✓ 4 large eggs
- ✓ 1 large red bell pepper, thinly sliced
- ✓ 1 large yellow bell pepper, thinly sliced
- ✓ 1 medium onion, thinly sliced
- ✓ 2 cups tomatoes, crushed or diced
- ✓ 2 garlic cloves, minced
- ✓ 2 tablespoons olive oil
- ✓ 1 teaspoon paprika
- ✓ 1/2 teaspoon cumin
- ✓ 1/4 teaspoon cayenne pepper (adjust to taste)
- ✓ Salt and black pepper to taste
- ✓ Fresh parsley, chopped (for garnish)
- ✓ Crumbled feta cheese (optional, for garnish)

Directions:

1. Heat olive oil in a large skillet over medium heat. Add onions and sauté until translucent.
2. Add the bell peppers and garlic. Continue to cook until peppers soften.
3. Stir in the tomatoes, paprika, cumin, cayenne pepper, salt, and black pepper. Let the mixture simmer for 10 minutes or until it thickens slightly.
4. Make four wells in the sauce using a spoon. Crack an egg into each well.
5. Cover the skillet and cook on low heat until the egg whites are set but yolks remain runny, about 5-7 minutes.
6. Remove from heat and garnish with fresh parsley and crumbled feta cheese if desired.
7. Serve hot with crusty bread or pita.

Nutrition: Calories: 270; Fat: 16g; Carbs: 19g; Protein: 13g; Sugar: 9g; Fiber: 5g

Equipment: Large skillet with lid; spatula.

Fresh Fruit Smoothie Bowl with Chopped Nuts

Prep time: 10 min　　**Total time:** 10 min
Cook time: 0 min　　**Servings:** 2

Ingredients:

- ✓ 2 bananas, 1 sliced for blending and the other for topping
- ✓ 1/2 cup strawberries, halved for blending and some for topping
- ✓ 1/2 cup blueberries, for blending and topping
- ✓ 1/2 cup kiwi slices, for topping

- ✓ 1 cup almond milk or any other preferred milk
- ✓ 1 tablespoon chia seeds
- ✓ 1 tablespoon honey or maple syrup (optional)
- ✓ 1/4 cup mixed chopped nuts (such as almonds, walnuts, and pistachios)
- ✓ A pinch of shredded coconut (optional)
- ✓ A few mint leaves for garnish (optional)

Directions:

1. In a blender, combine 1 sliced banana, half of the strawberries, half of the blueberries, almond milk, chia seeds, and honey or maple syrup if using. Blend until smooth and creamy.
2. Pour the smoothie mixture into two bowls.
3. Top each bowl with an even sprinkling of the remaining strawberries, blueberries, the other sliced banana, and kiwi slices.
4. Sprinkle with the chopped nuts and shredded coconut if desired.
5. Garnish with a few mint leaves for added freshness and a pop of color.
6. Serve immediately with a spoon and enjoy!

Nutrition: Calories: 290; Fat: 11g; Carbs: 46g; Protein: 7g; Sugar: 30g; Fiber: 9g

Equipment: Blender; Two serving bowls.

Nut Butter and Banana Whole Grain Crepes

Prep time: 10 min **Total time:** 25 min
Cook time: 15 min **Servings:** 2

Ingredients:

- ✓ 1/2 cup whole grain flour
- ✓ 1 egg
- ✓ 3/4 cup milk
- ✓ Pinch of salt
- ✓ 1 tablespoon unsalted butter, melted (for batter)
- ✓ Additional butter for frying
- ✓ 2 ripe bananas, sliced
- ✓ 4 tablespoons nut butter (e.g., almond or peanut butter)
- ✓ 1 tablespoon honey or maple syrup (optional)
- ✓ A sprinkle of cinnamon or cocoa powder (optional for garnish)
- ✓ Fresh berries for garnish (optional)

Directions:

1. In a mixing bowl, whisk together the whole grain flour, egg, milk, salt, and 1 tablespoon of melted butter until smooth. Let the batter rest for about 10 minutes.
2. Heat a non-stick frying pan over medium heat and lightly grease with butter.
3. Pour a ladle of batter into the center of the frying pan. Quickly tilt and rotate the pan to spread the batter thinly across the surface.
4. Cook until the underside of the crepe is golden brown, about 2 minutes. Flip and cook the other side.
5. Transfer the crepe to a plate and spread 2 tablespoons of the nut butter down the center of the crepe. Place banana slices on top. If desired, drizzle with honey or maple syrup.
6. Fold the crepe sides over the filling. Repeat with the remaining batter and filling.

7. Serve immediately, sprinkled with cinnamon or cocoa powder and garnished with fresh berries if desired.

Nutrition: Calories: 420; Fat: 21g; Carbs: 53g; Protein: 12g; Sugar: 18g; Fiber: 7g

Equipment: Mixing bowl; Whisk; Non-stick frying pan; Ladle.

Roasted Red Pepper and Feta Egg Muffins

Prep time: 15 min **Total time:** 40 min
Cook time: 25 min **Servings:** 2

Ingredients:

- 6 large eggs
- 1 roasted red pepper, finely chopped
- 1/2 cup feta cheese, crumbled
- 1/4 cup fresh parsley, chopped
- 1/4 cup milk
- 1/4 teaspoon black pepper
- 1/4 teaspoon salt
- Cooking spray or butter (for greasing)

Directions:

1. Preheat the oven to 375°F (190°C).
2. In a mixing bowl, whisk together the eggs, milk, salt, and black pepper until well combined.
3. Stir in the roasted red pepper, crumbled feta cheese, and chopped parsley.
4. Grease a muffin tin with cooking spray or butter.
5. Pour the egg mixture evenly into the muffin cups, filling each about 3/4 full.
6. Place the muffin tin in the oven and bake for 20-25 minutes, or until the egg muffins are firm and lightly golden on top.
7. Remove from the oven and let them cool slightly before serving.

Nutrition: Calories: 110; Fat: 8g; Carbs: 2g; Protein: 7g; Sugar: 1g; Fiber: 0.2g

Equipment: Mixing bowl; Whisk; Muffin tin.

SALAD RECIPES

Greek Salad with Feta and Olives

Prep time: 15 min **Total time:** 15 min
Cook time: 0 min **Servings:** 4

Ingredients:

- 4 large ripe tomatoes, cut into wedges
- 1 cucumber, sliced into half-moons
- 1 red onion, thinly sliced
- 1 green bell pepper, deseeded and sliced
- 1/2 cup Kalamata olives, pitted
- 200g feta cheese, crumbled or cut into blocks
- 1/4 cup extra virgin olive oil
- 2 tablespoons red wine vinegar
- 1 teaspoon dried oregano
- Salt and freshly ground black pepper, to taste

Directions:

1. In a large salad bowl, combine the tomatoes, cucumber, red onion, green bell pepper, and Kalamata olives.
2. In a small mixing bowl, whisk together the extra virgin olive oil, red wine vinegar, dried oregano, salt, and black pepper until well combined.
3. Pour the dressing over the salad and gently toss to coat all the ingredients.
4. Top the salad with crumbled or block feta cheese.
5. Serve immediately, garnishing with additional dried oregano if desired.

Nutrition: Calories: 260; Fat: 21g; Carbs: 14g; Protein: 7g; Sugar: 6g; Fiber: 3g

Equipment: Large salad bowl; Small mixing bowl; Whisk.

Tuna and White Bean Salad

Prep time: 20 min **Total time:** 20 min
Cook time: 0 min **Servings:** 4

Ingredients:

- 1 can (14 oz) white beans (such as cannellini or navy beans), drained and rinsed
- 1 can (5 oz) tuna in olive oil, drained and flaked
- 1 medium red onion, finely chopped
- 1 cup cherry tomatoes, halved
- 1 medium cucumber, sliced into rings and then quartered
- 1/2 cup feta cheese, crumbled
- 1/2 cup black olives, pitted and halved
- 1/4 cup extra virgin olive oil

- ✓ 2 tablespoons lemon juice or white wine vinegar
- ✓ Salt and freshly ground black pepper, to taste
- ✓ 1/2 teaspoon dried oregano (optional)
- ✓ 1 clove garlic, minced (optional)

Directions:

1. In a large mixing bowl, combine white beans, flaked tuna, chopped red onion, halved cherry tomatoes, quartered cucumber slices, crumbled feta cheese, and halved olives.
2. In a separate small bowl or jar, whisk together the extra virgin olive oil, lemon juice or vinegar, salt, black pepper, dried oregano (if using), and minced garlic (if using) to make the dressing.
3. Pour the dressing over the salad ingredients and gently mix until well combined.
4. Let the salad sit for 10 minutes to allow flavors to meld or refrigerate for later use.
5. Serve chilled or at room temperature.

Nutrition: Calories: 320; Fat: 15g; Carbs: 28g; Protein: 22g; Sugar: 4g; Fiber: 7g

Equipment: Large mixing bowl; Small bowl or jar; Whisk.

Lentil Salad with Tomatoes and Cucumber

Prep time: 15 min   **Total time:** 40 min
Cook time: 25 min   **Servings:** 4

Ingredients:

- ✓ 1 cup green or brown lentils, rinsed and drained
- ✓ 3 cups water
- ✓ 1 bay leaf (optional)
- ✓ 1/2 teaspoon salt, divided
- ✓ 1 cup cherry tomatoes, halved
- ✓ 1 medium cucumber, diced
- ✓ 1/4 cup red onion, sliced into thin half-moons
- ✓ 3 tablespoons extra-virgin olive oil
- ✓ 2 tablespoons fresh lemon juice
- ✓ 1/2 teaspoon freshly ground black pepper
- ✓ 1 tablespoon fresh mint, chopped (optional)

Directions:

1. Place the lentils in a saucepan with the water, bay leaf, and 1/4 teaspoon of salt. Bring to a boil, then reduce the heat and simmer for 20-25 minutes, or until lentils are tender but not mushy. Remove the bay leaf and drain any excess water.
2. Transfer the cooked lentils to a large mixing bowl and let them cool to room temperature.
3. Add the halved cherry tomatoes, diced cucumber, and thinly sliced red onion half-moons to the bowl with lentils.
4. In a small bowl or jug, whisk together the olive oil, fresh lemon juice, remaining 1/4 teaspoon of salt, and black pepper. Pour the dressing over the lentil mixture and toss to combine.
5. If using, stir in the chopped fresh mint.
6. Refrigerate the salad for about 30 minutes before serving to allow the flavors to meld together. Serve chilled.

Nutrition: Calories: 265; Fat: 11g; Carbs: 32g; Protein: 10g; Sugar: 4g; Fiber: 14g

Equipment: Medium saucepan; Large mixing bowl; Knife; Cutting board; Small bowl or jug; Whisk.

Cucumber and Radish Salad with Mint-Yogurt Dressing

Prep time: 15 min **Total time:** 15 min
Cook time: 0 min **Servings:** 4

Ingredients:

- 2 large cucumbers, thinly sliced
- 8 radishes, thinly sliced
- 1 cup plain Greek yogurt
- 2 tablespoons fresh mint, finely chopped
- 1 tablespoon lemon juice
- 1 garlic clove, minced
- Salt and freshly ground black pepper, to taste
- 1 tablespoon olive oil (optional for drizzling)
- Fresh dill, for garnish

Directions:

1. In a large mixing bowl, combine sliced cucumbers and radishes. Set aside.
2. In a separate smaller bowl, mix together Greek yogurt, finely chopped mint, lemon juice, and minced garlic. Season with salt and freshly ground black pepper to taste.
3. Drizzle the mint-yogurt dressing over the cucumber and radish mix. Toss gently until all the vegetables are coated with the dressing.
4. Optionally, you can drizzle a little olive oil over the salad for added richness.
5. Garnish the salad with fresh dill before serving.
6. Serve immediately or refrigerate for about 30 minutes before serving for a colder salad experience.

Nutrition: Calories: 75; Fat: 2g; Carbs: 9g; Protein: 4g; Sugar: 5g; Fiber: 1g

Equipment: Large mixing bowl, knife, chopping board.

Spinach and Strawberry Salad with Balsamic Vinaigrette

Prep time: 15 min **Total time:** 15 min
Cook time: 0 min **Servings:** 4

Ingredients:

- 4 cups fresh spinach leaves, washed and dried
- 2 cups strawberries, hulled and sliced
- 1/4 cup roasted walnuts, roughly chopped

- ✓ 1/4 cup feta cheese or goat cheese, crumbled
- ✓ 1/4 cup extra virgin olive oil
- ✓ 2 tablespoons balsamic vinegar
- ✓ 1 teaspoon honey or maple syrup
- ✓ 1 small garlic clove, minced (optional)
- ✓ Salt and freshly ground black pepper, to taste

Directions:

1. In a large salad bowl, combine the spinach leaves, sliced strawberries, chopped walnuts, and crumbled cheese.
2. In a separate small bowl or jar, whisk together the extra virgin olive oil, balsamic vinegar, honey or maple syrup, garlic (if using), salt, and black pepper until emulsified.
3. Just before serving, drizzle the vinaigrette over the salad and gently toss to combine, ensuring all ingredients are well-coated.
4. Serve immediately.

Nutrition: Calories: 210; Fat: 16g; Carbs: 13g; Protein: 5g; Sugar: 7g; Fiber: 3g

Equipment: Large salad bowl; Small bowl or jar; Whisk.

Quinoa and Roasted Vegetable Salad

Prep time: 20 min **Total time:** 45 min
Cook time: 25 min **Servings:** 4

Ingredients:

- ✓ 1 cup quinoa (uncooked)
- ✓ 2 cups water
- ✓ 1 medium zucchini, sliced into rings or half-rings
- ✓ 1 medium eggplant, sliced into rings or half-rings
- ✓ 1 carrot, chopped into pieces
- ✓ 1 yellow bell pepper, diced
- ✓ 1 red onion, chopped into wedges
- ✓ 3 tablespoons olive oil
- ✓ Salt and freshly ground black pepper, to taste
- ✓ 2 tablespoons fresh lemon juice
- ✓ 1/4 cup green onions (scallions), chopped

Directions:

1. Preheat your oven to 425°F (220°C).
2. In a large mixing bowl, combine the sliced zucchini, eggplant, carrot pieces, bell pepper, and red onion. Drizzle with 2 tablespoons of olive oil and season with salt and black pepper. Toss to coat.
3. Spread the vegetables on a baking sheet in an even layer and roast in the oven for 20-25 minutes, or until tender and slightly browned.
4. While the vegetables are roasting, rinse the quinoa under cold water. In a medium saucepan, bring 2 cups of water to a boil. Add the quinoa and a pinch of salt. Reduce the heat to low, cover, and cook for about 15 minutes, or until quinoa is tender and the water has been absorbed. Remove from heat and let it sit for 5 minutes, then fluff with a fork.
5. In a large bowl, combine the roasted vegetables with the cooked quinoa. Drizzle with the remaining 1 tablespoon of olive oil and fresh lemon juice. Toss to mix well.

6. Sprinkle with chopped green onions. Serve warm or at room temperature.

Nutrition: Calories: 295; Fat: 12g; Carbs: 38g; Protein: 8g; Sugar: 5g; Fiber: 6g

Equipment: Baking sheet; Large mixing bowl; Medium saucepan; Fork; Knife; Cutting board.

Tomato and Mozzarella Caprese

Prep time: 10 min **Total time:** 10 min
Cook time: 0 min **Servings:** 4

Ingredients:

- 4 large ripe tomatoes, sliced
- 1 pound fresh mozzarella cheese, sliced
- 1/4 cup fresh basil leaves
- 3 tablespoons extra-virgin olive oil
- 1 tablespoon balsamic vinegar
- Salt, to taste
- Freshly ground black pepper, to taste

Directions:

1. Arrange the tomato and mozzarella slices on a platter, alternating and overlapping them.
2. Tuck whole basil leaves in between the tomato and mozzarella slices.
3. Drizzle with the extra-virgin olive oil and balsamic vinegar.

4. Season with salt and freshly ground black pepper.
5. Serve immediately as a refreshing appetizer or side dish.

Nutrition: Calories: 320; Fat: 23g; Carbs: 7g; Protein: 22g; Sugar: 4g; Fiber: 1g

Equipment: Knife; Cutting board; Platter.

Orzo and Shrimp Salad with Lemon Dressing

Prep time: 15 min **Total time:** 35 min
Cook time: 20 min **Servings:** 4

Ingredients:

- 1 cup orzo pasta
- 1 pound large shrimp, peeled and deveined
- 1 tablespoon olive oil
- 1 cup cherry tomatoes, halved
- 1/2 cup cucumber, diced
- 1/4 cup red onion, finely chopped
- 1/4 cup green onions (scallions), thinly sliced
- 1/4 cup fresh dill, finely chopped
- 1/2 cup feta cheese, crumbled
- Zest and juice of 1 lemon
- 3 tablespoons extra-virgin olive oil
- 1 garlic clove, minced
- 1/2 teaspoon salt

- ✓ 1/4 teaspoon freshly ground black pepper

Directions:

1. Bring a large pot of salted water to a boil. Cook the orzo according to the package instructions until al dente. Drain and rinse under cold water to stop the cooking process. Set aside.
2. In a large skillet, heat the 1 tablespoon of olive oil over medium-high heat. Add the shrimp and cook for 1-2 minutes on each side, or until pink and opaque. Remove from the skillet and let cool.
3. In a large bowl, combine the cooked orzo, cooked shrimp, cherry tomatoes, cucumber, red onion, green onions, and dill.
4. For the dressing, whisk together the lemon zest, lemon juice, extra-virgin olive oil, minced garlic, salt, and pepper until emulsified.
5. Drizzle the dressing over the orzo and shrimp mixture. Toss well to combine. Gently fold in the crumbled feta cheese.
6. Refrigerate the salad for about 30 minutes before serving, allowing the flavors to meld together.

Nutrition: Calories: 365; Fat: 15g; Carbs: 38g; Protein: 26g; Sugar: 3g; Fiber: 2g

Equipment: Large pot; Colander; Large skillet; Large bowl; Whisk; Knife; Cutting board.

Beet and Arugula Salad with Goat Cheese

Prep time: 15 min **Total time:** 1 hour
Cook time: 45 min **Servings:** 4

Ingredients:

- ✓ 3 medium-sized beets, scrubbed and trimmed
- ✓ 4 cups arugula, washed and dried
- ✓ 1/2 cup goat cheese, crumbled
- ✓ 1/4 cup walnuts, toasted and roughly chopped
- ✓ 2 tablespoons extra-virgin olive oil
- ✓ 1 tablespoon balsamic vinegar
- ✓ 1 teaspoon honey or maple syrup
- ✓ 1/2 teaspoon freshly ground black pepper
- ✓ 1/4 teaspoon salt
- ✓ Zest of 1 lemon

Directions:

1. Preheat the oven to 400°F (200°C).
2. Wrap each beet individually in aluminum foil and place on a baking tray. Roast in the oven for 45 minutes or until the beets are tender and can be easily pierced with a fork.
3. Once cooked, remove the beets from the oven and let them cool. Once cooled, peel the skin off and slice them into wedges.
4. In a large bowl, combine the arugula, beet wedges, and half of the goat cheese.
5. In a small bowl, whisk together the olive oil, balsamic vinegar, honey or maple syrup, salt, and pepper to create the dressing.
6. Drizzle the dressing over the salad and toss gently to combine.
7. Serve the salad on plates, topped with the remaining goat cheese, toasted walnuts, and a sprinkle of lemon zest.

Nutrition: Calories: 220; Fat: 15g; Carbs: 16g; Protein: 7g; Sugar: 10g; Fiber: 3g

Equipment: Oven; Aluminum foil; Baking tray; Large bowl; Knife; Cutting board; Small bowl; Whisk.

Grilled Eggplant and Bell Pepper Salad

Prep time: 15 min **Total time:** 25 min
Cook time: 10 min **Servings:** 4

Ingredients:

- 2 medium eggplants, sliced into 1/2-inch thick rounds
- 2 large bell peppers (preferably one red and one yellow), seeded and quartered
- 3 tablespoons olive oil
- 2 garlic cloves, minced
- 1 tablespoon balsamic vinegar
- 1/4 cup fresh green onions (scallions), thinly sliced
- Salt and freshly ground black pepper, to taste

Directions:

1. Preheat the grill to medium-high heat.
2. Brush both sides of the eggplant slices and bell pepper quarters with olive oil.
3. Place the vegetables on the grill and cook for 4-5 minutes per side or until they have nice grill marks and are tender.
4. Once cooked, remove from the grill and let them cool slightly.
5. Once cooled, chop the grilled vegetables into bite-sized pieces and transfer them to a salad bowl.
6. In a small bowl, whisk together the minced garlic, balsamic vinegar, and remaining olive oil. Season with salt and pepper.
7. Drizzle the dressing over the grilled vegetables and toss gently to combine.
8. Sprinkle with thinly sliced green onions.
9. Serve immediately or chill for later.

Nutrition: Calories: 140; Fat: 9g; Carbs: 15g; Protein: 3g; Sugar: 8g; Fiber: 6g

Equipment: Grill; Brush; Salad bowl; Knife; Cutting board; Small bowl.

Mediterranean Couscous Salad

Prep time: 15 min **Total time:** 25 min
Cook time: 10 min **Servings:** 4

Ingredients:

- 1 cup couscous (preferably whole grain)
- 1 1/4 cup boiling water
- 1 tablespoon olive oil
- 1 cup cherry tomatoes, quartered

- ✓ 1 cup cucumber, diced
- ✓ 1/2 cup red bell pepper, diced
- ✓ 1/3 cup Kalamata olives, pitted and halved
- ✓ 1/4 cup fresh green onions (scallions), thinly sliced
- ✓ 1/4 cup fresh mint, finely chopped
- ✓ 1/4 cup fresh parsley, finely chopped
- ✓ 1/4 cup fresh dill, finely chopped
- ✓ 1 lemon, zest and juice
- ✓ Salt and freshly ground black pepper, to taste
- ✓ 1/4 cup crumbled feta cheese (optional)

Directions:

1. Place the couscous in a heatproof bowl. Pour the boiling water and olive oil over it, then cover and leave for 10 minutes until the couscous is soft and all the water is absorbed.
2. Using a fork, fluff up the couscous grains to separate them.
3. Transfer the couscous to a large salad bowl and allow it to cool slightly.
4. Add the quartered cherry tomatoes, cucumber, red bell pepper, Kalamata olives, and green onions to the bowl.
5. In a small mixing bowl, whisk together the lemon zest, lemon juice, mint, parsley, and dill. Season with salt and pepper.
6. Pour the dressing over the couscous and vegetable mixture and toss well to combine.
7. If desired, sprinkle crumbled feta cheese on top before serving.

Nutrition: Calories: 220; Fat: 7g; Carbs: 35g; Protein: 7g; Sugar: 4g; Fiber: 3g

Equipment: Heatproof bowl; Fork; Large salad bowl; Knife; Cutting board; Small mixing bowl.

Kale and Pomegranate Salad

Prep time: 20 min **Total time:** 20 min
Cook time: 0 min **Servings:** 4

Ingredients:

- ✓ 4 cups kale, stems removed, leaves torn into bite-sized pieces
- ✓ Seeds from 1 large pomegranate
- ✓ 1/2 cup walnuts, toasted and roughly chopped
- ✓ 1/4 cup crumbled feta cheese
- ✓ 1/4 cup thinly sliced red onion
- ✓ 2 tablespoons olive oil
- ✓ 1 tablespoon fresh lemon juice
- ✓ 1 teaspoon honey or maple syrup
- ✓ Salt and freshly ground black pepper, to taste

Directions:

1. In a large salad bowl, combine kale, pomegranate seeds, walnuts, and red onion.
2. In a small bowl, whisk together the olive oil, lemon juice, honey or maple syrup, salt, and pepper.
3. Pour the dressing over the kale mixture and toss to coat well.
4. Let the salad sit for about 5-10 minutes to allow the kale to soften slightly.
5. Sprinkle crumbled feta cheese on top before serving.

Nutrition: Calories: 250; Fat: 17g; Carbs: 20g; Protein: 7g; Sugar: 9g; Fiber: 3g

Equipment: Large salad bowl; Knife; Cutting board; Small mixing bowl; Whisk.

Roasted Cauliflower Salad with Tahini Dressing

Prep time: 15 min
Cook time: 25 min
Total time: 40 min
Servings: 4

Ingredients:

- 1 medium-sized cauliflower head, cut into florets
- 3 tablespoons olive oil
- Salt and freshly ground black pepper, to taste
- 1/4 cup tahini
- 2 tablespoons lemon juice
- 1 garlic clove, minced
- 3 tablespoons water (or more as needed for consistency)
- 1/2 cup chopped parsley
- 1/4 cup pomegranate seeds

Directions:

1. Preheat oven to 425°F (220°C).
2. Toss the cauliflower florets in olive oil and season with salt and pepper. Spread them on a baking sheet in a single layer.
3. Roast the cauliflower in the preheated oven for 20-25 minutes, or until golden brown and tender, stirring halfway through.
4. In a small bowl, whisk together tahini, lemon juice, minced garlic, and water. Adjust consistency with more water if needed and season with salt.
5. In a serving bowl, combine the roasted cauliflower, chopped parsley, and pomegranate seeds.
6. Drizzle the tahini dressing over the salad and gently toss to combine.
7. Serve immediately or refrigerate for later use.

Nutrition: Calories: 240; Fat: 18g; Carbs: 19g; Protein: 6g; Sugar: 6g; Fiber: 5g

Equipment: Baking sheet; Knife; Cutting board; Mixing bowls; Whisk.

Warm Potato Salad with Dill and Mustard

Prep time: 15 min
Cook time: 20 min
Total time: 35 min
Servings: 4

Ingredients:

- 1.5 lbs (680g) small potatoes, halved or quartered depending on size
- 3 tablespoons olive oil
- 2 tablespoons whole grain mustard
- 2 tablespoons apple cider vinegar

- ✓ 1/4 cup fresh dill, chopped
- ✓ 1/4 cup green onion, finely chopped
- ✓ Salt and freshly ground black pepper, to taste

Directions:

1. In a large pot of boiling salted water, cook the potatoes until just tender, about 15-20 minutes.
2. While the potatoes are cooking, in a small bowl, whisk together olive oil, mustard, apple cider vinegar, salt, and pepper.
3. Once the potatoes are cooked, drain and return them to the pot.
4. Pour the mustard dressing over the warm potatoes and toss gently to coat.
5. Add the finely chopped green onion and fresh dill, stirring to combine.
6. Transfer to a serving dish and serve warm.

Nutrition: Calories: 240; Fat: 9g; Carbs: 35g; Protein: 4g; Sugar: 3g; Fiber: 4g

Equipment: Large pot; Knife; Cutting board; Small mixing bowl; Whisk.

Marinated Zucchini Ribbon Salad with Pine Nuts and Goat Cheese

Prep time: 20 min
Cook time: 20 min
Total time: 40 min
Servings: 4

Marinating Time: 1 hour 20 min

Ingredients:

- ✓ 2 medium zucchinis
- ✓ 1/4 cup pine nuts, toasted
- ✓ 1/4 cup goat cheese (or feta), crumbled
- ✓ 2 tablespoons extra virgin olive oil
- ✓ 1 tablespoon lemon juice
- ✓ 1 garlic clove, minced
- ✓ 1 teaspoon honey or maple syrup
- ✓ Salt and freshly ground black pepper, to taste
- ✓ Fresh pea shoot microgreens, for garnish

Directions:

1. Using a vegetable peeler or mandolin, slice the zucchinis lengthwise into thin ribbons. Place them in a mixing bowl.
2. In a small bowl, combine the olive oil, lemon juice, minced garlic, honey or maple syrup, salt, and pepper. Whisk together until well combined.
3. Pour the dressing over the zucchini ribbons and toss gently to ensure all the ribbons are coated. Let the zucchini marinate in the refrigerator for at least 1 hour.
4. Once marinated, arrange the zucchini ribbons on a serving platter or individual plates.
5. Sprinkle the toasted pine nuts and crumbled goat cheese (or feta) over the top.
6. Garnish with fresh pea shoot microgreens.
7. Serve chilled and enjoy!

Nutrition: Calories: 140; Fat: 12g; Carbs: 8g; Protein: 4g; Sugar: 4g; Fiber: 1g

Equipment: Vegetable peeler or mandolin, mixing bowl, small whisking bowl.

FISH AND SEAFOOD RECIPES

Grilled Salmon with Lemon Herb Butter

Prep time: 15 min **Total time:** 25 min
Cook time: 10 min **Servings:** 4

Ingredients:

- 4 salmon fillets (about 6-8 oz each)
- Salt and freshly ground black pepper, to taste
- 1 tablespoon olive oil (for brushing)

For the Lemon Herb Butter:

- 1/2 cup unsalted butter, softened
- Zest of 1 lemon
- 2 tablespoons fresh lemon juice
- 2 tablespoons fresh parsley, finely chopped
- 1 tablespoon fresh dill, finely chopped
- 1 garlic clove, minced
- Salt and freshly ground black pepper, to taste

Directions:

1. Preheat the grill to medium-high heat.
2. While the grill is heating, prepare the lemon herb butter. In a mixing bowl, combine softened butter, lemon zest, lemon juice, chopped parsley, dill, and minced garlic. Season with salt and black pepper. Mix until all ingredients are well incorporated. Set aside.
3. Season salmon fillets on both sides with salt and pepper. Brush lightly with olive oil to prevent sticking to the grill.
4. Place salmon fillets on the grill and cook for 4-5 minutes on each side, or until the salmon easily flakes with a fork.
5. Once cooked, remove the salmon from the grill and place on serving plates.
6. While the salmon is still hot, top each fillet with a generous dollop of the lemon herb butter, allowing it to melt over the warm fish.
7. Serve immediately with additional lemon wedges, if desired.

Nutrition: Calories: 320; Fat: 20g; Carbs: 1g; Protein: 34g; Sugar: 0g; Fiber: 0g

Equipment: Grill, mixing bowl, knife, chopping board, brush.

Baked Cod with Olives and Tomatoes

Prep time: 10 min **Total time:** 30 min
Cook time: 20 min **Servings:** 4

Ingredients:

- 4 cod fillets (about 6-8 oz each)
- 1 cup cherry tomatoes, halved
- 1/2 cup Kalamata olives, pitted and halved
- 4 garlic cloves, minced
- 1/4 cup white wine (or chicken broth)
- 1 teaspoon dried oregano
- Salt and freshly ground black pepper, to taste
- 2 tablespoons capers
- 1 tablespoon olive oil

Directions:

1. Preheat your oven to 400°F (200°C).
2. In an oven-proof baking dish, spread olive oil. Place the cod fillets in the dish.
3. Sprinkle minced garlic, dried oregano, salt, and freshly ground black pepper over the cod. Scatter the halved cherry tomatoes, olives, and capers around the fish.
4. Drizzle the white wine (or chicken broth) over the ingredients in the dish.
5. Place the baking dish in the oven and bake for about 15-20 minutes, or until the cod becomes flaky and opaque.
6. Once cooked, remove from the oven.
7. Serve immediately.

Nutrition: Calories: 210; Fat: 5g; Carbs: 7g; Protein: 30g; Sugar: 2g; Fiber: 1g

Equipment: Oven, baking dish, knife, chopping board.

Shrimp and Garlic Linguine

Prep time: 15 min   **Total time:** 30 min
Cook time: 15 min   **Servings:** 4

Ingredients:

- 12 oz linguine pasta
- 1 lb large shrimp, peeled and deveined
- 4 garlic cloves, minced
- 1/4 cup extra-virgin olive oil
- 1/4 teaspoon red pepper flakes (optional for a bit of heat)
- 1/4 cup fresh parsley, finely chopped
- 1/4 cup white wine (optional)
- Salt and freshly ground black pepper, to taste
- Grated zest and juice of 1 lemon
- Freshly grated Parmesan cheese (optional for serving)

Directions:

1. Bring a large pot of salted water to a boil. Cook the linguine according to the package instructions until al dente. Reserve 1 cup of pasta water, then drain.
2. While the pasta is cooking, heat the olive oil in a large skillet over medium heat. Add the garlic and red pepper flakes, if using. Sauté for about 1 minute, or until fragrant.
3. Add the shrimp to the skillet. Season with salt and black pepper. Cook until the shrimp turns pink on both sides, about 2-3 minutes per side.
4. Pour in the white wine, if using, and let it simmer for a couple of minutes until reduced by half.
5. Add the drained linguine to the skillet. Toss to combine, adding reserved pasta water a little at a time to create a light sauce that coats the pasta.
6. Stir in the lemon zest, lemon juice, and chopped parsley. Toss until everything is well combined.

7. Serve hot, garnished with freshly grated Parmesan cheese, if desired.

Nutrition: Calories: 430; Fat: 12g; Carbs: 53g; Protein: 30g; Sugar: 2g; Fiber: 2g

Equipment: Large pot, colander, large skillet, knife, chopping board, grater.

Pan-Seared Tuna Steaks with Capers

Prep time: 10 min
Cook time: 7 min
Total time: 17 min
Servings: 4

Ingredients:

- 4 fresh tuna steaks (about 6-8 oz each)
- Salt and freshly ground black pepper, to taste
- 2 tablespoons olive oil
- 3 garlic cloves, minced
- 2 tablespoons capers, drained
- Juice of 1 lemon
- 1 tablespoon unsalted butter
- Lemon thyme sprigs (for garnish)

Directions:

1. Season the tuna steaks on both sides with salt and black pepper.
2. In a large skillet, heat the olive oil over medium-high heat.
3. Once the oil is hot, add the tuna steaks and sear for about 2-3 minutes on each side for medium-rare, or longer depending on desired doneness.
4. Remove the tuna steaks from the skillet and set aside on a plate.
5. In the same skillet, add the minced garlic and sauté for about 30 seconds until fragrant.
6. Stir in the capers and lemon juice, and let it simmer for about 1 minute.
7. Add the butter to the skillet and swirl around until melted and combined with the capers and lemon juice.
8. Return the tuna steaks to the skillet just to reheat for about 1 minute, spooning the caper sauce over them.
9. Remove from heat and serve the tuna steaks with the caper sauce drizzled on top, garnishing each steak with a sprig of lemon thyme.

Nutrition: Calories: 260; Fat: 11g; Carbs: 2g; Protein: 35g; Sugar: 0g; Fiber: 0g

Equipment: Large skillet, knife, chopping board, spoon.

Fish Stew with Saffron and White Wine

Prep time: 20 min
Cook time: 35 min
Total time: 55 min
Servings: 4

Ingredients:

- ✓ 4 fish fillets (such as cod, halibut, or sea bass), cut into chunks
- ✓ 2 tablespoons olive oil
- ✓ 1 large onion, finely chopped
- ✓ 3 garlic cloves, minced
- ✓ 1 red bell pepper, sliced
- ✓ 1 green bell pepper, sliced
- ✓ 1 can (14 oz) diced tomatoes
- ✓ 1/2 cup dry white wine
- ✓ 2 cups fish or vegetable broth
- ✓ A pinch of saffron threads, soaked in 2 tablespoons warm water
- ✓ 1 bay leaf
- ✓ Salt and freshly ground black pepper, to taste
- ✓ Fresh parsley, for garnish

Directions:

1. Heat the olive oil in a large pot over medium heat. Add the chopped onion and garlic, and sauté until translucent.
2. Add the red and green bell peppers to the pot and sauté for an additional 3 minutes.
3. Pour in the white wine and let it simmer until reduced by half.
4. Stir in the diced tomatoes, fish or vegetable broth, saffron with its soaking water, and bay leaf. Season with salt and pepper. Bring the mixture to a boil, then reduce the heat and let it simmer for about 15 minutes.
5. Gently add the fish chunks to the pot, ensuring they are submerged in the broth. Simmer for another 10 minutes, or until the fish is cooked through and easily flakes with a fork.
6. Discard the bay leaf.
7. Serve the stew in bowls, garnished with freshly chopped parsley.

Nutrition: Calories: 290; Fat: 8g; Carbs: 17g; Protein: 32g; Sugar: 5g; Fiber: 4g

Equipment: Large pot, knife, chopping board, spoon.

Stuffed Calamari with Rice and Herbs

Prep time: 30 min **Total time:** 55 min
Cook time: 25 min **Servings:** 4

Ingredients:

- ✓ 8 large calamari tubes and tentacles, cleaned
- ✓ 1 cup uncooked rice
- ✓ 2 tablespoons olive oil
- ✓ 1 small onion, finely chopped
- ✓ 3 garlic cloves, minced
- ✓ 1/4 cup fresh parsley, finely chopped
- ✓ 1/4 cup fresh dill, finely chopped
- ✓ 1/4 cup fresh mint, finely chopped
- ✓ Zest of 1 lemon
- ✓ Salt and freshly ground black pepper, to taste
- ✓ 1 cup chicken or vegetable broth
- ✓ Lemon wedges, for serving

Directions:

1. Cook the rice according to package instructions until it's al dente, then drain and set aside.
2. In a skillet, heat the olive oil over medium heat. Add the onion and garlic, and sauté until translucent.

3. Add the parsley, dill, mint, and lemon zest to the skillet and cook for another 2 minutes.
4. Combine the cooked rice with the herb mixture in the skillet, stirring well. Season with salt and pepper. This will be your filling.
5. Using a spoon, carefully stuff each calamari tube with the rice and herb mixture, ensuring not to overfill.
6. Secure the open end of each stuffed calamari with a toothpick.
7. In a separate pan or skillet, place the stuffed calamari tubes and tentacles. Pour the broth over them.
8. Cover and let simmer for about 20 minutes or until the calamari are tender.
9. Remove from heat and transfer the stuffed calamari tubes to serving plates, placing the tentacles beside the tubes.
10. Drizzle with a bit of the broth and serve with lemon wedges on the side.

Nutrition: Calories: 280; Fat: 5g; Carbs: 42g; Protein: 15g; Sugar: 1g; Fiber: 2g

Equipment: Skillet, pot, knife, chopping board, spoon, toothpicks.

Mussels in Tomato and Garlic Sauce

Prep time: 20 min
Cook time: 20 min
Total time: 40 min
Servings: 4

Ingredients:

- ✓ 2 pounds fresh mussels, cleaned and debearded
- ✓ 2 tablespoons olive oil
- ✓ 4 garlic cloves, minced
- ✓ 1 medium-sized yellow onion, finely chopped
- ✓ 1 can (14 oz) diced tomatoes
- ✓ 1/2 cup dry white wine
- ✓ 1/4 teaspoon red pepper flakes (optional for a hint of spice)
- ✓ Salt and freshly ground black pepper, to taste
- ✓ Fresh parsley leaves, chopped, for garnish

Directions:

1. Before cooking, rinse the mussels under cold water and remove any beards or debris. Discard any mussels that are cracked or don't close when tapped.
2. In a large pot or deep skillet, heat olive oil over medium heat. Add the minced garlic and chopped onion. Sauté until the onion becomes translucent and the garlic is fragrant, about 2-3 minutes.
3. Pour in the white wine and diced tomatoes (with their juices). Add red pepper flakes if using. Stir and bring the mixture to a simmer.
4. Add the mussels to the pot and cover with a lid. Allow the mussels to cook for about 5-7 minutes or until they have all opened. Make sure to discard any mussels that do not open after cooking.
5. Season the sauce with salt and freshly ground black pepper.
6. Transfer the mussels and sauce to serving dishes and garnish with chopped fresh parsley.

Nutrition: Calories: 220; Fat: 8g; Carbs: 14g; Protein: 22g; Sugar: 4g; Fiber: 2g

Equipment: Large pot or deep skillet, knife, chopping board, spoon.

Grilled Sardines with Olive and Tapenade

Prep time: 15 min **Total time:** 25 min
Cook time: 10 min **Servings:** 4

Ingredients:

- 12 fresh sardines, gutted and cleaned
- Salt and freshly ground black pepper, to taste
- 1 tablespoon olive oil (for brushing)
  For the Olive and Tapenade:
- 1 cup pitted black olives (like Kalamata)
- 2 garlic cloves, minced
- 2 tablespoons capers, drained
- 1 tablespoon fresh lemon juice
- 1/4 cup extra virgin olive oil
- 1/4 cup whole almonds
- 1 teaspoon anchovy paste (optional)
- Fresh mint leaves, for garnish

Directions:

1. Start by preparing the olive and almond tapenade. In a food processor, combine the black olives, garlic, capers, almonds, and lemon juice. Process until finely chopped.
2. While the processor is running, slowly drizzle in the olive oil until you get a paste-like consistency. Add the anchovy paste if using and blend until smooth. Set aside.
3. Preheat the grill to medium-high heat.
4. Season the sardines on both sides with salt and pepper. Lightly brush them with olive oil.
5. Place the sardines on the grill, and cook for about 3-4 minutes on each side, or until the skin is crispy and the flesh is opaque.
6. Remove the sardines from the grill and arrange them on a serving plate.
7. Spoon the olive and almond tapenade over the sardines or serve on the side. Garnish with fresh mint leaves.

Nutrition: Calories: 270; Fat: 19g; Carbs: 6g; Protein: 21g; Sugar: 1g; Fiber: 3g

Equipment: Grill, food processor, knife, chopping board, brush.

Roasted Trout with Almonds and Parsley

Prep time: 15 min **Total time:** 30 min
Cook time: 15 min **Servings:** 4

Ingredients:

- 4 trout fillets (about 6-8 oz each)
- Salt and freshly ground black pepper, to taste
- 2 tablespoons olive oil
- 1/2 cup sliced almonds
- 2 tablespoons unsalted butter

35

- ✓ 2 tablespoons fresh parsley, finely chopped
- ✓ 1 tablespoon fresh lemon juice

Directions:

1. Preheat the oven to 400°F (200°C).
2. Season the trout fillets on both sides with salt and pepper.
3. In a large, oven-safe skillet, heat the olive oil over medium heat. Once the oil is shimmering, add the trout fillets, skin-side down, and cook for about 2-3 minutes, or until the skin is golden brown.
4. Turn the fillets over and scatter the sliced almonds around the trout in the skillet.
5. Transfer the skillet to the preheated oven and roast for 7-9 minutes, or until the trout is cooked through and the almonds are golden brown and toasted.
6. Remove the skillet from the oven and place it back on the stovetop over low heat. Add the butter, and once it's melted, spoon the buttery almond mixture over the trout.
7. Sprinkle the trout with fresh parsley and drizzle with lemon juice.
8. Serve the trout fillets immediately, garnished with more parsley if desired.

Nutrition: Calories: 330; Fat: 23g; Carbs: 4g; Protein: 28g; Sugar: 1g; Fiber: 2g

Equipment: Oven, oven-safe skillet, knife, chopping board.

Clams with Chorizo and White Wine

Prep time: 15 min   **Total time:** 35 min
Cook time: 20 min   **Servings:** 4

Ingredients:

- ✓ 2 lbs (900g) fresh clams, cleaned and scrubbed
- ✓ 200g chorizo sausage, thinly sliced
- ✓ 1 tablespoon olive oil
- ✓ 1 onion, finely chopped
- ✓ 4 garlic cloves, minced
- ✓ 1/2 cup white wine (like Albariño or Sauvignon Blanc)
- ✓ 1/4 cup fresh parsley, chopped
- ✓ 1/2 teaspoon red pepper flakes (optional, for heat)
- ✓ Salt, to taste
- ✓ Freshly ground black pepper, to taste
- ✓ Crusty bread, for serving

Directions:

1. In a large skillet or pot, heat the olive oil over medium heat. Add the chorizo slices and cook until they release their oils and become slightly crispy, around 3-4 minutes.
2. Add the chopped onion to the skillet, and sauté until translucent, about 4-5 minutes.
3. Stir in the minced garlic and red pepper flakes (if using) and cook for another minute until fragrant.
4. Pour in the white wine and increase the heat to high. Let the mixture come to a boil.
5. Once boiling, add the cleaned clams to the skillet. Cover with a lid and let the clams steam for 5-7 minutes, or until they open. Discard any clams that do not open.
6. Season with salt and freshly ground black pepper. Stir in the chopped parsley.

7. Transfer the clams and chorizo mixture to serving bowls, making sure to include some of the flavorful broth.
8. Serve hot with crusty bread on the side to soak up the broth.

Nutrition: Calories: 290; Fat: 14g; Carbs: 8g; Protein: 25g; Sugar: 1g; Fiber: 0.5g

Equipment: Large skillet or pot with lid, knife, chopping board, stirring spoon.

Shrimp and Artichoke Paella

Prep time: 20 min **Total time:** 60 min
Cook time: 40 min **Servings:** 4

Ingredients:

- 1 lb (450g) large shrimp, peeled and deveined
- 1 cup Arborio rice or paella rice
- 2 tablespoons olive oil
- 1 onion, finely chopped
- 3 garlic cloves, minced
- 1 red bell pepper, diced
- 1/2 teaspoon saffron threads
- 1/4 teaspoon smoked paprika
- 1/4 teaspoon cayenne pepper (optional, for heat)
- 2 cups chicken or vegetable broth
- 1 cup canned or jarred artichoke hearts, quartered
- 1/4 cup fresh parsley, chopped
- 1 lemon, cut into wedges, for serving
- Salt and freshly ground black pepper, to taste

Directions:

1. In a large paella pan or wide skillet, heat the olive oil over medium heat. Add the onions and red bell pepper, and sauté until they are soft and translucent, about 5 minutes.
2. Stir in the garlic and cook for another minute until fragrant.
3. Add the rice to the pan, stirring to coat with the oil and vegetables. Cook for 2-3 minutes until the rice is slightly translucent.
4. Stir in the saffron threads, smoked paprika, and cayenne pepper (if using). Pour in the chicken or vegetable broth and season with salt and black pepper. Gently mix to ensure all ingredients are well combined.
5. Arrange the artichoke quarters and shrimp evenly over the rice. Reduce the heat to low, cover, and let the paella simmer for about 25-30 minutes, or until the rice is tender and the shrimp are pink and cooked through.
6. Remove from heat and let the paella stand covered for about 5 minutes. This allows the flavors to meld.
7. Garnish with fresh parsley and serve with lemon wedges on the side.

Nutrition: Calories: 360; Fat: 8g; Carbs: 49g; Protein: 24g; Sugar: 3g; Fiber: 3g

Equipment: Paella pan or wide skillet, knife, chopping board, stirring spoon.

Spicy Octopus Salad

Prep time: 25 min **Total time:** 65 min
Cook time: 40 min **Servings:** 4

Ingredients:

- 500g fresh octopus, cleaned and tentacles separated
- 2 red chili peppers, thinly sliced

- ✓ 1 cucumber, thinly sliced into half-moons
- ✓ 1 red bell pepper, thinly sliced
- ✓ 2 spring onions, thinly sliced
- ✓ 150g cherry tomatoes, halved
- ✓ Juice of 2 limes
- ✓ 3 tablespoons olive oil
- ✓ 1 tablespoon rice vinegar
- ✓ 1 teaspoon honey
- ✓ 1 garlic clove, minced
- ✓ Salt and freshly ground black pepper, to taste
- ✓ Fresh cilantro leaves, for garnish

Directions:

1. In a large pot of boiling salted water, add the octopus and cook until tender, about 35-40 minutes. Once cooked, drain and allow to cool. Once cooled, slice the tentacles into bite-sized pieces.
2. In a large mixing bowl, combine the cooked octopus pieces, chili peppers, cucumber, red bell pepper, spring onions, and halved cherry tomatoes.
3. In a smaller bowl, whisk together lime juice, olive oil, rice vinegar, honey, minced garlic, salt, and pepper. Pour this dressing over the octopus and vegetables in the larger bowl. Toss to coat everything in the dressing.
4. Chill the salad in the refrigerator for at least 15 minutes before serving.
5. Serve the salad garnished with fresh cilantro leaves.

Nutrition: Calories: 230; Fat: 10g; Carbs: 12g; Protein: 20g; Sugar: 5g; Fiber: 3g

Equipment: Large pot, mixing bowl, knife, chopping board, whisk, small bowl.

Baked Halibut with Fennel, Cherry Tomatoes, and Olives

Prep time: 20 min **Total time:** 45 min
Cook time: 25 min **Servings:** 4

Ingredients:

- ✓ 4 halibut fillets (about 6-8 oz each)
- ✓ 2 tablespoons olive oil
- ✓ 1 fennel bulb, thinly sliced
- ✓ 1 cup cherry tomatoes
- ✓ 1/2 cup green olives, pitted
- ✓ 1/2 cup kalamata olives, pitted
- ✓ 3 garlic cloves, minced
- ✓ Zest and juice of 1 lemon
- ✓ Salt and freshly ground black pepper, to taste

Directions:

1. Preheat the oven to 375°F (190°C).

2. In a large ovenproof skillet or pan, heat 1 tablespoon of olive oil over medium heat. Add the sliced fennel and sauté until it's slightly softened and golden, about 5-7 minutes.
3. Add the minced garlic to the skillet and sauté for an additional minute until fragrant.
4. Scatter the whole cherry tomatoes, green olives, and kalamata olives over the fennel and garlic mixture.
5. Place the halibut fillets on top of the vegetables in the skillet. Drizzle the remaining olive oil over the fish, then season each fillet with salt, pepper, and lemon zest.
6. Pour the lemon juice over the top of the fish and vegetables.
7. Transfer the skillet to the oven and bake for 15-20 minutes, or until the halibut easily flakes with a fork.
8. Remove from the oven and let it rest for a few minutes before serving.
9. Serve the halibut on plates, ensuring each serving has a mix of fennel, cherry tomatoes, and olives.

Equipment: Oven, ovenproof skillet or pan, knife, chopping board, zester.

Nutrition: Calories: 270; Fat: 11g; Carbs: 10g; Protein: 34g; Sugar: 4g; Fiber: 3g

Lemon and Herb Grilled Swordfish

Prep time: 15 min **Total time:** 25 min
Cook time: 10 min **Servings:** 4

Ingredients:

✓ 4 swordfish steaks (about 6-8 oz each)
✓ 3 tablespoons olive oil
✓ Zest and juice of 2 lemons
✓ 2 garlic cloves, minced
✓ 2 tablespoons fresh parsley, finely chopped
✓ 1 tablespoon fresh rosemary, finely chopped
✓ 1 tablespoon fresh thyme, finely chopped
✓ Salt and freshly ground black pepper, to taste

Directions:

1. In a bowl, mix together olive oil, lemon zest, lemon juice, minced garlic, parsley, rosemary, and thyme. Season the mixture with salt and pepper, stirring to combine.
2. Place the swordfish steaks in a large dish or Ziploc bag. Pour the herb marinade over the fish, ensuring each piece is well coated. Let the fish marinate for at least 10-15 minutes.
3. Preheat the grill to medium-high heat.
4. Once the grill is hot, remove the swordfish from the marinade and place it on the grill. Cook for 4-5 minutes on each side or until the fish is opaque and easily flakes with a fork.
5. Transfer the grilled swordfish to serving plates and drizzle with any remaining marinade if desired.
6. Serve immediately, garnished with additional lemon wedges and herbs if preferred.

Nutrition: Calories: 280; Fat: 15g; Carbs: 3g; Protein: 30g; Sugar: 1g; Fiber: 1g

Equipment: Grill, mixing bowl, knife, chopping board, large dish or Ziploc bag.

POULTRY AND MEAT RECIPES

Grilled Chicken with Lemon and Parsley

Prep time: 20 min
Cook time: 15 min
Total time: 35 min
Servings: 4

Ingredients:

- 4 boneless chicken breasts
- Zest and juice of 2 lemons, plus extra lemon slices for garnish
- 3 tablespoons olive oil
- 4 garlic cloves, minced
- 2 tablespoons fresh parsley, chopped, plus extra for garnish
- Salt and freshly ground black pepper, to taste
- Fresh basil leaves, for garnish

Directions:

1. In a bowl, combine the lemon zest, lemon juice, olive oil, minced garlic, chopped parsley, salt, and black pepper. Mix well to form a marinade.
2. Place the chicken breasts in a large dish or zip-top bag and pour the marinade over them. Ensure each breast is well-coated. Marinate for at least 1 hour in the refrigerator, turning the chicken occasionally.
3. Preheat the grill to medium-high heat.
4. Remove the chicken from the marinade and discard the excess marinade. Grill the chicken breasts for 6-7 minutes on each side or until fully cooked and nicely charred.
5. Once cooked, transfer the chicken breasts to a plate and let them rest for a few minutes.
6. Serve the grilled chicken garnished with additional fresh parsley, basil leaves, and lemon slices.

Nutrition: Calories: 260; Fat: 10g; Carbs: 5g; Protein: 35g; Sugar: 1g; Fiber: 1g

Equipment: Grill, mixing bowl, large dish or zip-top bag, tongs, plate.

Turkey Meatballs with Tomato Sauce

Prep time: 25 min
Cook time: 40 min
Total time: 1 h 5 min
Servings: 4

Ingredients:

For the Turkey Meatballs:
- 1 lb ground turkey
- 1/4 cup breadcrumbs
- 1/4 cup grated Parmesan cheese
- 1 large egg
- 2 cloves garlic, minced

- ✓ 2 tablespoons fresh parsley, finely chopped
- ✓ Salt and freshly ground black pepper, to taste

For the Tomato Sauce:
- ✓ 1 can (28 oz) crushed tomatoes
- ✓ 1 small onion, finely chopped
- ✓ 1 red bell pepper, finely chopped
- ✓ 2 cloves garlic, minced
- ✓ 2 tablespoons olive oil
- ✓ 1 teaspoon dried oregano
- ✓ 1 teaspoon dried basil
- ✓ Salt and freshly ground black pepper, to taste

Directions:

1. **For the Meatballs:** In a large mixing bowl, combine ground turkey, breadcrumbs, grated Parmesan, egg, minced garlic, chopped parsley, salt, and black pepper. Mix until all ingredients are well incorporated.
2. Shape the mixture into 1.5-inch meatballs and set aside.
3. Heat a large skillet or pan over medium heat and add a drizzle of olive oil. Brown the meatballs on all sides, ensuring they are not cooked through. Once browned, remove and set aside.
4. **For the Tomato Sauce:** In the same skillet, add 2 tablespoons of olive oil. Sauté the finely chopped onions and red bell pepper until they are soft and translucent, then add minced garlic and cook for an additional 2 minutes.
5. Pour in the crushed tomatoes and add dried oregano and basil. Season with salt and pepper. Bring the sauce to a simmer.
6. Gently place the browned meatballs into the sauce, ensuring they are submerged. Cover and let them simmer for 20-25 minutes until the meatballs are cooked through.
7. Taste the sauce and adjust the seasoning if needed.
8. Serve the turkey meatballs with a generous helping of tomato sauce.

Garnish with additional fresh parsley and grated Parmesan if desired.

Nutrition: Calories: 325; Fat: 15g; Carbs: 20g; Protein: 28g; Sugar: 7g; Fiber: 4g

Equipment: Large mixing bowl, skillet or pan, spatula, measuring spoons and cups.

Roast Lamb with Rosemary and Garlic

Prep time: 20 min **Total time:** 1 h 50 min
Cook time: 1 h 30 min **Servings:** 6

Ingredients:

- ✓ 1 bone-in leg of lamb (about 4-5 lbs)
- ✓ 5 garlic cloves, minced
- ✓ 3 tablespoons fresh rosemary, finely chopped
- ✓ 3 tablespoons olive oil
- ✓ Salt and freshly ground black pepper, to taste
- ✓ 1 cup beef or chicken broth (for roasting)

Directions:

1. Preheat the oven to 325°F (165°C).
2. In a bowl, combine the minced garlic, chopped rosemary, olive oil, salt, and black pepper to create a paste.
3. Clean the leg of lamb and pat it dry with paper towels. With a sharp knife, make several small incisions over the surface of the lamb.

4. Rub the rosemary-garlic paste over the entire surface of the lamb, ensuring that some of the mixture goes into the incisions.
5. Place the leg of lamb in a roasting pan. Pour the broth into the bottom of the pan to prevent the drippings from burning and to create a flavorful base for a sauce or gravy, if desired.
6. Roast the lamb in the preheated oven for about 1.5 hours or until the internal temperature reaches 135°F (57°C) for medium-rare. Adjust the cooking time if you prefer your lamb more well-done.
7. Once cooked, remove the lamb from the oven and let it rest for 15 minutes before carving. This allows the juices to redistribute throughout the meat.
8. Slice and serve with your favorite side dishes.

Nutrition: Calories: 410; Fat: 28g; Carbs: 2g; Protein: 35g; Sugar: 0g; Fiber: 0g

Equipment: Oven, roasting pan, mixing bowl, knife, meat thermometer.

Baked Chicken with Olives and Capers

Prep time: 20 min   **Total time:** 1 h 5 min
Cook time: 45 min   **Servings:** 4

Ingredients:

- 4 chicken thighs or breasts (bone-in, skin-on)
- Salt and freshly ground black pepper, to taste
- 2 tablespoons olive oil
- 1 medium onion, finely chopped
- 4 cloves garlic, minced
- 1/2 cup green olives, pitted and sliced
- 1/4 cup capers, rinsed and drained
- 1 cup chicken broth
- 2 tablespoons fresh lemon juice
- 1 teaspoon dried oregano
- Fresh parsley, finely chopped for garnish

Directions:

1. Preheat your oven to 375°F (190°C).
2. Season the chicken pieces on both sides with salt and freshly ground black pepper.
3. In a large ovenproof skillet or pan, heat the olive oil over medium-high heat. Add the chicken pieces, skin-side down, and sear until the skin is golden and crispy, about 5 minutes. Flip the chicken and sear the other side for another 3 minutes. Remove the chicken from the skillet and set aside.
4. In the same skillet, add the chopped onion and sauté until translucent, about 2-3 minutes. Add the minced garlic, olives, and capers. Sauté for an additional 2 minutes.
5. Pour in the chicken broth and lemon juice, and sprinkle in the dried oregano. Stir everything together and bring the mixture to a simmer.
6. Return the seared chicken to the skillet, skin-side up. Transfer the skillet to the preheated oven.
7. Bake for 30-35 minutes or until the chicken is cooked through and the internal temperature reaches 165°F (74°C).
8. Once cooked, remove the skillet from the oven. Garnish the chicken with freshly chopped parsley before serving.

Nutrition: Calories: 320; Fat: 18g; Carbs: 6g; Protein: 31g; Sugar: 2g; Fiber: 2g

Equipment: Oven, large ovenproof skillet or pan, spatula, knife, chopping board, measuring spoons and cups.

Pork Chops Roasted Fennel and Tomatoes

Prep time: 15 min **Total time:** 45 min
Cook time: 30 min **Servings:** 4

Ingredients:

- 4 pork chops, bone-in (about 6-8 oz each)
- Salt and freshly ground black pepper, to taste
- 2 tablespoons olive oil, divided
- 2 large fennel bulbs, trimmed and cut into wedges
- 2 cups cherry tomatoes
- 2 garlic cloves, minced
- 3-4 fresh thyme sprigs
- Zest of 1 lemon
- 2 tablespoons fresh dill, chopped

Directions:

1. Preheat the oven to 400°F (200°C).
2. Season pork chops on both sides with salt and black pepper.
3. In a large oven-safe skillet, heat 1 tablespoon of olive oil over medium-high heat. Add the pork chops and sear for about 4-5 minutes on each side until they have a nice golden crust. Remove the chops and set them aside.
4. In the same skillet, add the remaining olive oil. Add fennel wedges and sauté for a few minutes until they start to brown.
5. Add cherry tomatoes, minced garlic, thyme sprigs, and lemon zest to the skillet. Stir to combine.
6. Place the seared pork chops back into the skillet, nestling them amongst the fennel and tomatoes.
7. Transfer the skillet to the preheated oven and roast for about 15-20 minutes, or until the pork chops are cooked through and the fennel is tender.
8. Remove from the oven and sprinkle with freshly chopped dill. Let rest for a few minutes before serving.

Nutrition: Calories: 310; Fat: 14g; Carbs: 10g; Protein: 35g; Sugar: 5g; Fiber: 4g

Equipment: Oven, oven-safe skillet, knife, chopping board.

Grilled Beef Kebabs with Tzatziki

Prep time: 25 min **Total time:** 40 min
Cook time: 15 min **Servings:** 4

Marinating Time: 2 hours

Ingredients:

- 500g beef sirloin, cut into 1-inch cubes
- 1 tablespoon olive oil
- 2 garlic cloves, minced
- 1 teaspoon dried oregano
- 1 teaspoon paprika
- Juice of 1 lemon
- Salt and freshly ground black pepper, to taste
- Wooden skewers, soaked in water for 30 minutes

For the Tzatziki:
- 1 cup Greek yogurt
- 1 medium cucumber, peeled, seeded, and finely grated
- 2 garlic cloves, minced

- ✓ 1 tablespoon fresh dill, finely chopped
- ✓ 1 tablespoon fresh mint, finely chopped
- ✓ Juice of 1/2 lemon
- ✓ Salt, to taste
- ✓ Olive oil, for drizzling

Directions:

1. In a large mixing bowl, combine olive oil, minced garlic, oregano, paprika, lemon juice, salt, and black pepper. Mix well to form a marinade.
2. Add beef cubes to the marinade, ensuring they are well coated. Cover and refrigerate for at least 2 hours, preferably overnight.
3. Preheat grill to medium-high heat.
4. Thread the marinated beef cubes onto soaked wooden skewers.
5. Grill the beef kebabs for 6-7 minutes on each side or until they reach your desired level of doneness.
6. While the beef is grilling, prepare the tzatziki sauce. In a bowl, mix Greek yogurt, grated cucumber, minced garlic, dill, mint, and lemon juice. Season with salt and drizzle with a touch of olive oil.
7. Once the beef kebabs are grilled, serve immediately with the tzatziki sauce on the side.

Nutrition: Calories: 320; Fat: 15g; Carbs: 8g; Protein: 35g; Sugar: 5g; Fiber: 1g

Equipment: Grill, mixing bowls, wooden skewers, grater.

Stuffed Chicken Breasts with Spinach and Feta

Prep time: 20 min **Total time:** 45 min
Cook time: 25 min **Servings:** 4

Ingredients:

- ✓ 4 boneless, skinless chicken breasts
- ✓ 200g fresh spinach
- ✓ 100g feta cheese, crumbled
- ✓ 2 garlic cloves, minced
- ✓ 1 tablespoon olive oil
- ✓ Salt and freshly ground black pepper, to taste
- ✓ 1/2 teaspoon dried oregano
- ✓ 4 toothpicks or kitchen twine

Directions:

1. Preheat oven to 200°C (400°F).
2. In a large skillet, heat olive oil over medium heat. Add minced garlic and sauté until fragrant, about 1 minute.
3. Add fresh spinach to the skillet and cook until wilted, about 3-4 minutes. Remove from heat and allow to cool slightly.
4. Once cooled, mix in the crumbled feta cheese.
5. Carefully create a pocket in each chicken breast by making a horizontal

slice, ensuring not to cut all the way through.
6. Stuff each chicken breast with the spinach and feta mixture. Secure the openings with toothpicks or tie with kitchen twine.
7. Season the stuffed chicken breasts with salt, black pepper, and dried oregano.
8. Transfer the chicken breasts to a baking dish and bake in the preheated oven for 20-25 minutes or until chicken is fully cooked and no longer pink inside.
9. Once cooked, remove the toothpicks or twine before serving.

Nutrition: Calories: 290; Fat: 12g; Carbs: 3g; Protein: 40g; Sugar: 1g; Fiber: 1g

Equipment: Large skillet, baking dish, toothpicks or kitchen twine.

Braised Rabbit with Red Wine and Herbs

Prep time: 20 min   **Total time:** 2 h 20 min
Cook time: 2 hours   **Servings:** 4

Marinating Time: 2 hours

Ingredients:

- 1 whole rabbit, cut into serving pieces
- 750ml red wine (preferably a robust variety like Cabernet Sauvignon or Merlot)
- 3 garlic cloves, minced
- 2 large onions, finely chopped
- 2 carrots, sliced into rounds
- 1 celery stalk, chopped
- 2 bay leaves
- 3 sprigs fresh thyme
- 3 sprigs fresh rosemary
- 500ml chicken stock
- 2 tablespoons olive oil
- Salt and freshly ground black pepper, to taste

Directions:

1. In a large bowl, marinate the rabbit pieces in red wine, garlic, and herbs (thyme, rosemary, and bay leaves) for at least 2 hours, or overnight in the refrigerator for best results.
2. Preheat your oven to 160°C (320°F).
3. In a large Dutch oven or heavy-bottomed pot, heat olive oil over medium heat. Remove the rabbit from the marinade (reserving the wine and herbs) and season with salt and pepper. Brown the rabbit pieces on all sides.
4. Remove the rabbit and set aside. In the same pot, add onions, carrots, and celery. Sauté until the onions become translucent.
5. Return the rabbit pieces to the pot. Add the reserved wine, herbs, and chicken stock.
6. Cover the pot and transfer it to the preheated oven. Braise for 1.5 to 2 hours or until the rabbit is tender and easily pulls apart.
7. Once done, remove the rabbit pieces from the pot and strain the sauce if desired. Return the sauce to the pot and simmer until slightly reduced.
8. Serve the rabbit pieces covered with the sauce.

Nutrition: Calories: 480; Fat: 12g; Carbs: 12g; Protein: 40g; Sugar: 4g; Fiber: 2g

Equipment: Large bowl, Dutch oven or heavy-bottomed pot, oven.

Herb-Crusted Rack of Lamb

Prep time: 15 min **Total time:** 40 min
Cook time: 25 min **Servings:** 4

Ingredients:

- 2 racks of lamb (about 7-8 ribs each)
- 2 tablespoons Dijon mustard
- 3 garlic cloves, minced
- 1 cup fresh breadcrumbs
- 1/4 cup fresh parsley, finely chopped
- 2 tablespoons fresh rosemary, finely chopped
- 2 tablespoons fresh thyme, finely chopped
- 2 tablespoons olive oil
- Salt and freshly ground black pepper, to taste

Directions:

1. Preheat your oven to 200°C (400°F).
2. In a bowl, mix together breadcrumbs, parsley, rosemary, thyme, garlic, salt, and pepper.
3. Season each rack of lamb with salt and pepper. In a large ovenproof skillet, heat olive oil over medium-high heat. Add the lamb, fat side down, and sear until golden brown, about 4 minutes. Flip and sear the other side for another 4 minutes.
4. Remove the skillet from heat. Brush the top side of each rack with Dijon mustard. Press the breadcrumb mixture onto the mustard.
5. Transfer the skillet to the preheated oven and roast for about 15-20 minutes for medium-rare, or until desired doneness. Use a meat thermometer to check: 60°C (140°F) for medium-rare.
6. Once done, remove from the oven and let it rest for 5 minutes before slicing between ribs.

Nutrition: Calories: 510; Fat: 35g; Carbs: 12g; Protein: 38g; Sugar: 1g; Fiber: 1g

Equipment: Oven, large ovenproof skillet, mixing bowl, meat thermometer.

Lemon and Garlic Roast Chicken

Prep time: 20 min **Total time:** 1 h 35 min
Cook time: 1 h 15 min **Servings:** 4-6

Ingredients:

- 1 whole chicken (about 4-5 lbs)
- 4 garlic cloves, minced
- 1 large lemon, zested and sliced
- 2 tablespoons olive oil
- 1 teaspoon fresh thyme leaves (or 1/2 teaspoon dried)
- Salt and freshly ground black pepper, to taste
- 2 additional lemons, quartered, for garnish

Directions:

1. Preheat your oven to 190°C (375°F).

2. Rinse the chicken and pat dry with paper towels. Place the chicken in a roasting pan.
3. In a small bowl, mix together the olive oil, minced garlic, lemon zest, thyme, salt, and pepper to form a paste.
4. Rub the paste evenly over the chicken, ensuring some goes under the skin as well.
5. Inside the chicken cavity, stuff the sliced lemon.
6. Place the chicken in the oven and roast for about 1 hour and 15 minutes, or until the chicken is golden brown and the juices run clear. Baste occasionally with the pan juices.
7. Once done, remove from the oven and let it rest for about 10 minutes before carving.
8. Serve with quartered lemons for garnish.

Nutrition: Calories: 420; Fat: 28g; Carbs: 5g; Protein: 35g; Sugar: 1g; Fiber: 1g

Equipment: Oven, roasting pan, mixing bowl, paper towels.

Beef and Eggplant Moussaka

Prep time: 30 min **Total time:** 1 h 30 min
Cook time: 1 hour **Servings:** 6-8

Ingredients:

✓ 2 large eggplants, thinly sliced
✓ 500g ground beef
✓ 1 large onion, finely chopped
✓ 3 garlic cloves, minced
✓ 1 can (400g) diced tomatoes
✓ 2 tablespoons tomato paste
✓ 1/4 cup red wine (optional)
✓ 2 teaspoons dried oregano
✓ 1 teaspoon ground cinnamon
✓ Salt and freshly ground black pepper, to taste
✓ 3 tablespoons olive oil
✓ 50g butter
✓ 50g all-purpose flour
✓ 500ml milk
✓ 100g grated Parmesan cheese
✓ 1 egg, beaten

Directions:

1. Preheat your oven to 190°C (375°F).
2. In a skillet, heat 2 tablespoons of olive oil. Fry the eggplant slices until golden on each side. Set aside on paper towels to drain excess oil.
3. In the same skillet, add the remaining olive oil and sauté onions until translucent. Add the garlic and ground beef, cooking until browned.
4. Stir in the diced tomatoes, tomato paste, red wine (if using), oregano, and cinnamon. Season with salt and pepper. Simmer for 15-20 minutes until the mixture thickens.
5. For the béchamel sauce: In a saucepan, melt the butter. Stir in the flour until smooth. Gradually add the milk, stirring constantly until thickened. Remove from heat, and then stir in half the Parmesan cheese and the beaten egg. Season with salt and pepper.
6. In a baking dish, layer half the eggplant slices, then spread half the beef mixture on top. Repeat with another layer of eggplant and beef.
7. Pour the béchamel sauce over the top, spreading evenly. Sprinkle with the remaining Parmesan cheese.

8. Bake in the preheated oven for 45 minutes, or until the top is golden brown and bubbly.
9. Allow the moussaka to rest for 10 minutes before serving.

Nutrition: Calories: 450; Fat: 28g; Carbs: 25g; Protein: 23g; Sugar: 8g; Fiber: 6g

Equipment: Oven, skillet, saucepan, baking dish.

Pan-Seared Duck Breasts with Cherry Sauce

Prep time: 15 min   **Total time:** 40 min
Cook time: 25 min   **Servings:** 4

Ingredients:

- 2 duck breasts (around 200g each), skin on
- Salt and freshly ground black pepper, to taste
- 200g fresh cherries, pitted and halved
- 1/2 cup red wine
- 2 tablespoons balsamic vinegar
- 2 tablespoons honey
- 1 shallot, finely chopped
- 2 cloves garlic, minced
- 1 sprig fresh rosemary
- 1 tablespoon unsalted butter

Directions:

1. Preheat your oven to 200°C (400°F).
2. Score the skin of the duck breasts in a crisscross pattern without cutting into the meat. Season both sides with salt and pepper.
3. Place duck breasts skin-side down in a cold skillet. Turn the heat to medium and render the fat until the skin is crispy and golden brown, about 6-8 minutes.
4. Turn the duck breasts over and sear for another 2 minutes. Transfer them to the preheated oven for 5-7 minutes for medium-rare. Remove from the oven and let them rest for 5 minutes.
5. In the same skillet, remove excess duck fat, leaving about 2 tablespoons. Add the shallot and garlic, sautéing until translucent.
6. Add the cherries, red wine, balsamic vinegar, honey, and rosemary sprig. Simmer until the sauce is reduced by half and has thickened, approximately 10 minutes.
7. Remove the rosemary sprig and whisk in the butter to make the sauce silky.
8. Slice the duck breasts and serve with the cherry sauce drizzled on top.

Nutrition: Calories: 360; Fat: 18g; Carbs: 20g; Protein: 24g; Sugar: 14g; Fiber: 1g

Equipment: Oven, skillet, knife.

Slow-Roasted Pork Shoulder with Sage

Prep time: 20 min   **Total time:** 4 h 20 min
Cook time: 4 hours   **Servings:** 6

Ingredients:

- 2 kg pork shoulder, bone-in
- 2 tablespoons olive oil
- 1 head of garlic, cloves separated and peeled
- 15 fresh sage leaves
- Salt and freshly ground black pepper, to taste
- 2 onions, sliced
- 1 cup chicken broth

Directions:

1. Preheat your oven to 150°C (300°F).
2. Pat the pork shoulder dry with paper towels. Rub the pork all over with olive oil, followed by a generous seasoning of salt and pepper.
3. Make small incisions all over the pork shoulder using a sharp knife. Insert garlic cloves and sage leaves into each incision.
4. Place the sliced onions in a roasting pan, forming a bed for the pork. Rest the pork shoulder on top of the onions.
5. Pour the chicken broth around the pork.
6. Cover the roasting pan with aluminum foil and transfer to the oven.
7. Roast the pork shoulder for about 4 hours, or until the meat is tender and easily pulls apart.
8. Once cooked, remove the pork from the oven and let it rest for about 15 minutes before serving.

Nutrition: Calories: 450; Fat: 28g; Carbs: 5g; Protein: 42g; Sugar: 2g; Fiber: 1g

Equipment: Oven, roasting pan, sharp knife, aluminum foil.

Mediterranean Meatloaf with Sun-Dried Tomatoes

Prep time: 20 min **Total time:** 1 h 15 min
Cook time: 55 min **Servings:** 6

Ingredients:

- 500g ground beef
- 500g ground lamb
- 1 cup breadcrumbs
- 2 large eggs, beaten
- 1/2 cup sun-dried tomatoes, finely chopped
- 1/2 cup kalamata olives, pitted and chopped
- 1 medium onion, finely diced
- 4 cloves garlic, minced
- 1 teaspoon dried oregano
- 1/2 teaspoon dried rosemary
- Salt and freshly ground black pepper, to taste
- 1/4 cup fresh parsley, chopped
- 100g feta cheese, crumbled
- Olive oil for drizzling

Directions:

1. Preheat the oven to 180°C (350°F).
2. In a large mixing bowl, combine the ground beef, ground lamb, breadcrumbs, eggs, sun-dried tomatoes, olives, onion, garlic, oregano, rosemary,

parsley, and feta cheese. Mix until just combined, being careful not to over-mix.
3. Season the mixture with salt and black pepper.
4. Transfer the meat mixture to a loaf pan or shape it into a loaf on a lined baking sheet.
5. Drizzle the top of the meatloaf with olive oil.
6. Place the meatloaf in the preheated oven and bake for approximately 55 minutes, or until the meatloaf is fully cooked through and has a golden-brown crust.
7. Once cooked, remove the meatloaf from the oven and allow it to rest for 10 minutes before slicing.

Nutrition: Calories: 460; Fat: 28g; Carbs: 15g; Protein: 38g; Sugar: 4g; Fiber: 2g

Equipment: Oven, loaf pan or lined baking sheet, large mixing bowl.

Chicken and Chorizo Paella

Prep time: 20 min
Cook time: 40 min
Total time: 1 hour
Servings: 6

Ingredients:

- 400g chicken thighs, boneless and skinless, cut into bite-sized pieces
- 200g chorizo sausage, sliced
- 2 cups Arborio or paella rice
- 1 large onion, finely diced
- 4 cloves garlic, minced
- 1 red bell pepper, diced
- 1 yellow bell pepper, diced
- 4 cups chicken broth
- 1/2 teaspoon saffron threads (or turmeric for color)
- 1 teaspoon smoked paprika
- 1 cup frozen peas, thawed
- 2 tomatoes, diced
- 1/4 cup fresh parsley, chopped
- 1 lemon, sliced into wedges
- Olive oil
- Salt and freshly ground black pepper, to taste

Directions:

1. In a large paella pan or wide skillet, heat olive oil over medium heat. Add the chicken pieces and chorizo slices. Cook until the chicken is browned and the chorizo releases its oils.
2. Add the onion, garlic, and bell peppers. Sauté until the onions are translucent and the peppers soften.
3. Stir in the rice, ensuring each grain gets coated with the oils and flavors in the pan.
4. Pour in the chicken broth and sprinkle in the saffron threads (or turmeric) and smoked paprika. Season with salt and pepper. Mix well.
5. Allow the mixture to simmer for about 25-30 minutes, or until the rice is almost cooked through. Do not stir too often as this is a characteristic of traditional paella.
6. Scatter the peas and diced tomatoes over the top of the paella. Continue cooking for another 5-7 minutes, or until the rice is fully cooked and has absorbed the broth.
7. Garnish with fresh parsley and lemon wedges.

Nutrition: Calories: 490; Fat: 22g; Carbs: 48g; Protein: 28g; Sugar: 4g; Fiber: 3g

Equipment: Paella pan or wide skillet, stirring spoon.

VEGETABLE RECIPES

Ratatouille with Fresh Basil

Prep time: 25 min
Cook time: 40 min
Total time: 1 h 5 min
Servings: 6

Ingredients:

- ✓ 1 eggplant, diced into 1-inch cubes
- ✓ 2 zucchinis, sliced
- ✓ 1 red bell pepper, diced
- ✓ 1 yellow bell pepper, diced
- ✓ 2 medium-sized tomatoes, diced
- ✓ 1 large red onion, chopped
- ✓ 3 cloves garlic, minced
- ✓ 3 tablespoons olive oil
- ✓ 1/4 cup fresh basil, finely chopped + some whole leaves for garnish
- ✓ 1 teaspoon dried thyme
- ✓ 1 teaspoon dried oregano
- ✓ Salt and freshly ground black pepper, to taste

Directions:

1. In a large skillet or pot, heat the olive oil over medium heat.
2. Add the onions and garlic, sautéing until translucent and fragrant, approximately 3 minutes.
3. Incorporate the eggplant, zucchini, and bell peppers. Sauté for about 10 minutes or until the vegetables start to get tender.
4. Mix in the tomatoes, thyme, oregano, salt, and pepper. Reduce the heat to low and let the mixture simmer for 25-30 minutes, occasionally stirring.
5. Once the vegetables are soft and the flavors melded, remove from heat. Stir in the finely chopped basil.
6. Transfer the Ratatouille to a serving dish and garnish with whole basil leaves.

Nutrition: Calories: 110; Fat: 5g; Carbs: 15g; Protein: 2g; Sugar: 8g; Fiber: 5g

Equipment: Large skillet or pot, knife, chopping board, stirring spoon, serving dish.

Baked Eggplant with Tomato and Mozzarella

Prep time: 15 min
Cook time: 40 min
Total time: 55 min
Servings: 4

Ingredients:

- ✓ 2 medium-sized eggplants, sliced into 1/2-inch rounds
- ✓ 3 large tomatoes, sliced into 1/2-inch rounds
- ✓ 200g mozzarella cheese, thinly sliced
- ✓ 1/4 cup grated Parmesan cheese
- ✓ 1/4 cup fresh basil leaves, torn, plus extra for garnish
- ✓ 3 cloves garlic, minced
- ✓ 3 tablespoons olive oil
- ✓ Salt and freshly ground black pepper, to taste

- ✓ 1 teaspoon dried oregano

Directions:

1. Preheat your oven to 375°F (190°C).
2. Brush both sides of the eggplant slices with olive oil and season with salt and pepper. Place them on a baking sheet lined with parchment paper.
3. Bake the eggplant slices in the preheated oven for 15-20 minutes, flipping once, until they are slightly tender and lightly browned.
4. In a baking dish, start layering the ingredients: Begin with a layer of eggplant, followed by a layer of tomato slices, then mozzarella slices. Sprinkle some minced garlic, torn basil, oregano, and a touch of salt and pepper between the layers.
5. Continue layering until all ingredients are used up, finishing with a layer of mozzarella on top. Sprinkle the top with grated Parmesan cheese.
6. Place the baking dish in the oven and bake for 20-25 minutes, or until the cheese is melted and bubbly, and the top is golden brown.
7. Remove from the oven and let it sit for a few minutes before serving. Garnish with additional fresh basil leaves.

Nutrition: Calories: 310; Fat: 20g; Carbs: 18g; Protein: 15g; Sugar: 10g; Fiber: 6g

Equipment: Baking sheet, parchment paper, baking dish, knife, chopping board, brush.

Zucchini Noodles with Pesto and Pine Nuts

Prep time: 15 min **Total time:** 20 min
Cook time: 5 min **Servings:** 4

Ingredients:

- ✓ 4 medium-sized zucchinis
- ✓ 1 cup fresh basil leaves
- ✓ 1/3 cup pine nuts, plus extra for garnish
- ✓ 2 cloves garlic
- ✓ 1/2 cup grated Parmesan cheese
- ✓ 1/3 cup extra virgin olive oil
- ✓ Salt and freshly ground black pepper, to taste
- ✓ 1 tablespoon lemon juice
- ✓ 1/4 cup cherry tomatoes, halved (for garnish)

Directions:

1. Using a spiralizer or vegetable peeler, turn zucchinis into thin noodle-like strands. Set aside.
2. In a skillet over medium heat, toast the pine nuts until they are golden and fragrant. Be careful, as they can burn quickly. Remove from the skillet and set aside.
3. In a food processor, combine the fresh basil, garlic, Parmesan cheese, toasted pine nuts, and lemon juice. Process until coarsely chopped.
4. While the processor is running, slowly drizzle in the olive oil until the pesto is smooth. Season with salt and black pepper to taste.
5. In a large mixing bowl, toss the zucchini noodles with the prepared pesto until well coated.
6. Serve the zucchini noodles on plates, garnishing with extra pine nuts and halved cherry tomatoes.

Nutrition: Calories: 290; Fat: 25g; Carbs: 10g; Protein: 8g; Sugar: 4g; Fiber: 3g

Equipment: Spiralizer or vegetable peeler, skillet, food processor, mixing bowl.

Stuffed Bell Peppers with Rice and Herbs

Prep time: 20 min **Total time:** 1 h 5 min
Cook time: 45 min **Servings:** 4

Ingredients:

- 4 large bell peppers (red, yellow, or green), tops removed and seeds scooped out
- 1 cup uncooked brown rice
- 2 cups chicken or vegetable broth
- 1 small onion, finely diced
- 2 cloves garlic, minced
- 1/4 cup fresh parsley, chopped
- 1/4 cup fresh basil, chopped
- 1/4 cup fresh mint, chopped, plus extra leaves for garnish
- 2 tablespoons olive oil
- Salt and freshly ground black pepper, to taste
- 200g mozzarella cheese, grated or thinly sliced

Directions:

1. Preheat your oven to 375°F (190°C).
2. In a medium-sized pot, bring the chicken or vegetable broth to a boil. Add the brown rice, reduce the heat to low, cover, and simmer for 30-35 minutes, or until the rice is cooked and has absorbed the broth.
3. While the rice is cooking, heat olive oil in a skillet over medium heat. Sauté the onions until translucent. Add the garlic and cook for another 1-2 minutes.
4. Once the rice is ready, combine it with the sautéed onions and garlic, fresh parsley, basil, and mint. Season with salt and pepper and mix well.
5. Stuff each bell pepper with the rice and herb mixture, pressing down gently to pack the filling.
6. Place the stuffed bell peppers in a baking dish, standing upright.
7. Top each stuffed bell pepper with mozzarella cheese.
8. Cover the baking dish with aluminum foil and bake in the preheated oven for 25-30 minutes, or until the bell peppers are tender and the cheese is melted and slightly golden.
9. Remove from the oven and let sit for a few minutes before serving. Garnish with additional fresh mint leaves and bell pepper stems for a decorative touch.

Nutrition: Calories: 390; Fat: 15g; Carbs: 52g; Protein: 14g; Sugar: 7g; Fiber: 6g

Equipment: Medium-sized pot, skillet, baking dish, knife, chopping board.

Mediterranean Spaghetti Squash with Feta

Prep time: 15 min **Total time:** 1 hour
Cook time: 45 min **Servings:** 4

Ingredients:

- 1 medium-sized spaghetti squash (about 2-3 pounds)
- 2 tbsp extra virgin olive oil
- 2 garlic cloves, minced
- 1 small red onion, thinly sliced

- 1 cup cherry tomatoes, cut into quarters
- 1 cup black olives, sliced into rings
- 1/2 cup crumbled feta cheese
- 1/4 cup fresh parsley, chopped
- 1/2 tsp sea salt
- 1/4 tsp freshly ground black pepper
- 1/4 tsp red pepper flakes (optional)

Directions:

1. Preheat the oven to 400°F (200°C).
2. Cut the spaghetti squash in half lengthwise and scoop out the seeds.
3. Place the two halves, cut side down, on a baking sheet lined with parchment paper.
4. Bake for 40-45 minutes, or until the flesh of the squash is tender and can easily be scraped with a fork into spaghetti-like strands.
5. While the squash is roasting, heat the olive oil in a large skillet over medium heat.
6. Add the garlic and red onion. Sauté until the onion is translucent.
7. Add the quartered cherry tomatoes and olive rings to the skillet and cook for another 5-7 minutes.
8. Once the squash is done roasting, let it cool slightly, then use a fork to scrape out the flesh into spaghetti-like strands.
9. Add the spaghetti squash strands to the skillet and toss with the tomato and olive mixture.
10. Season with salt, black pepper, and red pepper flakes.
11. Stir in the crumbled feta cheese and parsley. Toss until combined and heated through.
12. Serve warm.

Nutrition: Calories: 210; Fat: 12g; Carbs: 23g; Protein: 6g; Sugar: 7g; Fiber: 5g

Equipment: Baking sheet, parchment paper, large skillet.

Roasted Butternut Squash with Sage

Prep time: 15 min **Total time:** 55 min
Cook time: 40 min **Servings:** 4

Ingredients:

- 1 medium butternut squash, peeled, seeded, and diced into 1-inch cubes
- 2 tbsp extra virgin olive oil
- 1/4 tsp freshly ground black pepper
- 1/2 tsp sea salt
- 12 fresh sage leaves, roughly chopped
- 2 garlic cloves, minced
- A drizzle of maple syrup (optional)
- A sprinkle of red chili flakes (optional)

Directions:

1. Preheat the oven to 400°F (200°C).
2. In a large mixing bowl, toss the butternut squash cubes with olive oil, salt, black pepper, minced garlic, and half of the chopped sage.
3. Spread the squash evenly on a baking sheet lined with parchment paper.
4. Roast in the oven for 30-40 minutes, stirring occasionally, until the squash is tender and has a golden-brown hue.
5. Five minutes before the squash is done, sprinkle the remaining sage over it for added freshness.
6. Once out of the oven, drizzle with maple syrup if desired, and sprinkle with chili flakes for a hint of heat.
7. Serve warm as a side dish.

Nutrition: Calories: 120; Fat: 7g; Carbs: 17g; Protein: 1g; Sugar: 4g; Fiber: 3g

Equipment: Baking sheet, parchment paper, large mixing bowl.

Grilled Portobello Mushrooms with Garlic

Prep time: 15 min **Total time:** 25 min
Cook time: 10 min **Servings:** 4

Ingredients:

- 4 large portobello mushrooms
- 4 garlic cloves, finely minced
- 3 tbsp extra virgin olive oil
- 1 tbsp balsamic vinegar
- Salt and freshly ground black pepper, to taste
- Fresh parsley, finely chopped (for garnish)

Directions:

1. Preheat the grill to medium-high heat.
2. In a small mixing bowl, whisk together the minced garlic, olive oil, balsamic vinegar, salt, and black pepper.
3. Brush the mixture over both sides of the portobello mushrooms, ensuring the garlic is evenly distributed.
4. Place the mushrooms, gill side down, on the grill. Grill for about 5 minutes on each side or until tender and slightly charred.
5. Remove the mushrooms from the grill and place them on a serving platter.
6. Garnish with freshly chopped parsley.
7. Serve immediately.

Nutrition: Calories: 90; Fat: 7g; Carbs: 5g; Protein: 2g; Sugar: 2g; Fiber: 1g

Equipment: Grill, small mixing bowl, pastry brush.

Baked Artichokes with Lemon and Thyme

Prep time: 20 min **Total time:** 1 h 10 min
Cook time: 50 min **Servings:** 4

Ingredients:

- 4 whole artichokes
- 2 lemons, zested and juiced
- 4 garlic cloves, minced
- 3 tbsp extra virgin olive oil
- 4 sprigs fresh thyme
- Salt and freshly ground black pepper, to taste
- 1 cup water

Directions:

1. Preheat the oven to 375°F (190°C).
2. Trim the stems off the artichokes so they can sit flat. Snip the tips of the artichoke leaves using scissors.
3. In a bowl, mix together the lemon zest, lemon juice, minced garlic, olive oil, salt, and black pepper.
4. Gently spread the artichoke leaves apart and drizzle the lemon-garlic mixture inside, ensuring that it gets between the leaves.
5. Place the thyme sprigs on top of each artichoke.
6. Set the artichokes in a baking dish. Pour the water into the bottom of the dish.
7. Cover the baking dish tightly with aluminum foil.
8. Bake in the preheated oven for about 50 minutes, or until the artichokes are tender and can be easily pierced with a fork.
9. Remove from the oven and let cool slightly before serving.

Nutrition: Calories: 130; Fat: 10g; Carbs: 12g; Protein: 3g; Sugar: 1g; Fiber: 5g

Equipment: Oven, baking dish, scissors, mixing bowl.

Roasted Asparagus with Parmesan

Prep time: 10 min **Total time:** 30 min
Cook time: 20 min **Servings:** 4

Ingredients:

- 500g fresh asparagus, woody ends trimmed
- 2 tablespoons olive oil
- Salt and freshly ground black pepper, to taste
- 50g Parmesan cheese, freshly grated
- 1 lemon, zested (optional)
- 1 tablespoon lemon wedges, for serving

Directions:

1. Preheat the oven to 200°C (390°F).
2. Spread the asparagus out in a single layer on a baking sheet. Drizzle with olive oil and toss the asparagus to ensure they are evenly coated.
3. Season the asparagus with salt and freshly ground black pepper.
4. Roast in the oven for 12-15 minutes, or until the asparagus are tender but still have a slight crunch.
5. Once out of the oven, while still hot, sprinkle the grated Parmesan cheese over the top of the asparagus.

6. Optionally, sprinkle with lemon zest for added freshness.
7. Serve immediately, garnished with lemon wedges on the side.

Nutrition: Calories: 120; Fat: 9g; Carbs: 5g; Protein: 6g; Sugar: 2g; Fiber: 2g

Equipment: Baking sheet, grater, knife, chopping board, zester (if using).

Sautéed Spinach with Garlic and Lemon

Prep time: 10 min **Total time:** 15 min
Cook time: 5 min **Servings:** 4

Ingredients:

- 400g fresh spinach, washed and trimmed
- 2 tablespoons olive oil
- 3 garlic cloves, thinly sliced
- Zest of 1 lemon
- 2 tablespoons lemon juice
- Salt and freshly ground black pepper, to taste
- 1 tablespoon lemon wedges, for serving

Directions:

1. Heat the olive oil in a large skillet over medium heat. Once hot, add the sliced garlic, and sauté until it's fragrant but not browned, about 1 minute.
2. Add the fresh spinach to the skillet. Using tongs, turn the spinach in the hot oil, allowing it to wilt. This should take 2-3 minutes.
3. Once the spinach has wilted, add the lemon zest and lemon juice. Toss to combine.
4. Season with salt and freshly ground black pepper to taste. Remove from heat.
5. Serve immediately, garnished with lemon wedges.

Nutrition: Calories: 65; Fat: 7g; Carbs: 3g; Protein: 1g; Sugar: 0g; Fiber: 1g

Equipment: Large skillet, tongs, knife, chopping board, zester or fine grater.

Broccoli and Feta Sauté

Prep time: 10 min **Total time:** 25 min
Cook time: 15 min **Servings:** 4

Ingredients:

- 2 tbsp extra-virgin olive oil
- 2 garlic cloves, minced
- 4 cups broccoli florets
- 1/4 cup water
- 1/2 cup feta cheese, crumbled
- Zest of 1 lemon
- Juice of 1/2 lemon
- Salt and pepper to taste
- Red pepper flakes (optional, for a touch of heat)

Directions:

1. In a large skillet, heat olive oil over medium heat. Add the minced garlic and sauté for about 1 minute or until fragrant.
2. Add the broccoli florets to the skillet and sauté for about 5 minutes, until they start to turn a vibrant green.
3. Pour in the water and cover the skillet with a lid. Allow the broccoli to steam for about 5-7 minutes or until tender.
4. Once the broccoli is cooked, add the lemon zest, lemon juice, and crumbled feta cheese. Stir well.
5. Season with salt, pepper, and red pepper flakes if using. Stir and cook for an additional 2 minutes.
6. Transfer to a serving dish and serve warm.

Nutrition: Calories: 135; Fat: 9g; Carbs: 10g; Protein: 6g; Sugar: 3g; Fiber: 3g

Equipment: Skillet, knife, chopping board, stirring spoon, zester.

Chickpea and Vegetable Curry

Prep time: 15 min
Cook time: 30 min
Total time: 45 min
Servings: 4

Ingredients:

- 2 cans (800g) chickpeas, drained and rinsed
- 2 tablespoons olive oil or coconut oil
- 1 large onion, diced
- 3 garlic cloves, minced
- 1 tablespoon ginger, grated
- 2 medium carrots, sliced
- 1 bell pepper, diced (any color)
- 200g green beans, trimmed and halved
- 1 medium zucchini, sliced into half-moons
- 200g fresh spinach, roughly chopped
- 400ml canned coconut milk
- 2 tablespoons curry powder
- 1 teaspoon ground turmeric
- 1 teaspoon ground cumin
- 1/2 teaspoon chili powder (adjust to preference)
- Salt and freshly ground black pepper, to taste
- Lime wedges, for serving

Directions:

1. In a large pot or skillet, heat the oil over medium heat. Add the onions, garlic, and ginger. Sauté until the onions are translucent, about 3-5 minutes.
2. Add the carrots, bell pepper, green beans, and zucchini. Cook for another 5 minutes until the vegetables begin to soften slightly.
3. Stir in the curry powder, turmeric, cumin, and chili powder. Sauté for another minute until the spices are fragrant.
4. Pour in the coconut milk and add the chickpeas to the pot. Stir well, ensuring that all the ingredients are mixed.
5. Cover the pot, reduce heat to low, and let the curry simmer for 15 minutes.
6. Mix in the chopped spinach and let it cook until just wilted, about 3-5 minutes.
7. Season with salt and black pepper. Adjust the seasoning as necessary.
8. Serve the curry in bowls, accompanied with lime wedges on the side.

Nutrition: Calories: 450; Fat: 25g; Carbs: 47g; Protein: 17g; Sugar: 8g; Fiber: 13g

Equipment: Large pot or skillet, knife, chopping board, grater, can opener, stirring spoon.

Mediterranean Stuffed Zucchini Boats

Prep time: 20 min
Cook time: 35 min
Total time: 55 min
Servings: 4-6

Ingredients:

- 4 medium-sized zucchinis
- 1 cup cooked quinoa
- 1 cup cherry tomatoes, quartered
- 1/2 cup cooked chickpeas (canned or freshly boiled)
- 1/4 cup red onion, finely chopped
- 2 cloves garlic, minced
- 2 tbsp extra-virgin olive oil
- 1/4 cup feta cheese, crumbled
- 1 tbsp fresh basil, finely chopped
- Salt and pepper to taste

Directions:

1. Preheat the oven to 375°F (190°C).
2. Halve the zucchinis lengthwise and scoop out the insides, leaving about a 1/4-inch thick border to create a boat.
3. In a skillet, heat olive oil over medium heat. Add red onion and garlic and sauté until translucent.
4. Add the chopped zucchini flesh to the skillet and cook for 2-3 minutes.
5. Stir in the quinoa, cherry tomatoes, and chickpeas. Season with salt and pepper. Cook for another 2 minutes.
6. Remove from heat and mix in the feta cheese and basil.
7. Fill each zucchini boat with the mixture.
8. Place the zucchini boats in a baking dish and cover with foil.
9. Bake for 25 minutes. Remove the foil and bake for an additional 10 minutes.

Nutrition: Calories: 180; Fat: 8g; Carbs: 24g; Protein: 8g; Sugar: 4g; Fiber: 5g

Equipment: Skillet, baking dish, knife, chopping board, spoon, foil.

SNACK RECIPES

Greek Tzatziki Sauce with Whole Grain Pita

Prep time: 15 min
Cook time: 0 min
Total time: 15 min
Servings: 6

Ingredients:

- 2 cups Greek yogurt, full-fat
- 1 medium cucumber, peeled, seeded, and finely grated
- 3 cloves garlic, minced
- 1 tablespoon fresh dill, chopped
- 2 tablespoons fresh lemon juice
- 1 tablespoon olive oil
- 1/2 teaspoon salt
- 1/4 teaspoon black pepper
- 6 whole grain pita breads

Directions:

1. Start by squeezing out as much moisture as possible from the grated cucumber. This can be done by using a cheesecloth or a sieve and pressing down.
2. In a mixing bowl, combine the Greek yogurt, drained cucumber, minced garlic, fresh dill, lemon juice, olive oil, salt, and pepper. Stir until well combined.
3. Refrigerate the tzatziki sauce for at least 1 hour before serving to allow the flavors to meld.
4. When ready to serve, take the tzatziki sauce out of the refrigerator and give it a good stir.
5. Serve the tzatziki sauce with whole grain pita bread on the side.

Nutrition: Calories: 215; Fat: 4g; Carbs: 33g; Protein: 12g; Sugar: 5g; Fiber: 5g

Equipment: Mixing bowl; Cheesecloth or sieve.

Tomato and Mozzarella Skewers with Basil

Prep time: 15 min
Cook time: 0 min
Total time: 15 min
Servings: 6

Ingredients:

- 24 cherry tomatoes, washed
- 24 mini mozzarella balls (bocconcini)
- 24 fresh basil leaves
- 2 tablespoons extra-virgin olive oil
- 1 tablespoon balsamic vinegar
- 1/2 teaspoon sea salt
- 1/4 teaspoon freshly ground black pepper
- 12 small wooden skewers

Directions:

1. Begin by assembling the skewers. Start with a cherry tomato, followed by a fresh basil leaf (folded in half if it's large), and then a mini mozzarella ball. Repeat the sequence once more on the same skewer.
2. Lay the assembled skewers on a serving platter.
3. In a small bowl, whisk together the extra-virgin olive oil, balsamic vinegar, sea salt, and black pepper.
4. Drizzle the olive oil and balsamic mixture over the assembled skewers.
5. Serve immediately or refrigerate until ready to serve. If refrigerating, consider drizzling the olive oil and balsamic mixture just before serving for better presentation.

Nutrition: Calories: 125; Fat: 9g; Carbs: 5g; Protein: 7g; Sugar: 2g; Fiber: 1g

Equipment: Small bowl; Whisk; Serving platter; Small wooden skewers.

Stuffed Olives with Feta Cheese

Prep time: 20 min **Total time:** 20 min
Cook time: 0 min **Servings:** 6

Ingredients:

- 24 large green olives, pitted
- 100 grams feta cheese, crumbled
- 1 tablespoon extra-virgin olive oil
- 1 teaspoon lemon zest
- 1/4 teaspoon red chili flakes (optional)
- 1/4 teaspoon freshly ground black pepper

Directions:

1. In a mixing bowl, combine the crumbled feta cheese, olive oil, lemon zest, red chili flakes (if using), and black pepper. Mix until the ingredients are well combined and form a paste-like consistency.
2. Carefully stuff each pitted olive with the feta cheese mixture using a small spoon or a piping bag. Ensure that the filling is snug inside the olive but not overflowing.
3. Arrange the stuffed olives on a serving platter or in a bowl.
4. Refrigerate for at least 1 hour to allow the flavors to meld. Serve chilled.

Nutrition: Calories: 80; Fat: 7g; Carbs: 2g; Protein: 2g; Sugar: 1g; Fiber: 1g

Equipment: Mixing bowl; Small spoon or piping bag; Serving platter or bowl.

Hummus with Vegetable Sticks

Prep time: 15 min **Total time:** 15 min
Cook time: 0 min **Servings:** 4

Ingredients:

- ✓ 1 can (400 grams) chickpeas, drained and rinsed
- ✓ 2 garlic cloves, minced
- ✓ 3 tablespoons tahini
- ✓ 3 tablespoons lemon juice
- ✓ 2 tablespoons extra-virgin olive oil
- ✓ 1/2 teaspoon ground cumin
- ✓ Salt, to taste
- ✓ Water, as needed to achieve desired consistency
- ✓ Fresh parsley, for garnish (optional)
- ✓ 1 carrot, peeled and cut into sticks
- ✓ 1 cucumber, cut into sticks
- ✓ 1 bell pepper, cut into sticks
- ✓ 1 celery stalk, cut into sticks

Directions:

1. In a food processor, combine the chickpeas, minced garlic, tahini, lemon juice, olive oil, ground cumin, and salt.
2. Process the mixture until smooth. If the hummus is too thick, add water, one tablespoon at a time, until the desired consistency is achieved.
3. Transfer the hummus to a serving bowl.
4. Drizzle with a bit of olive oil and garnish with fresh parsley, if using.
5. Arrange the cut vegetables around the hummus or in a separate plate for dipping.

Nutrition: Calories: 225; Fat: 11g; Carbs: 27g; Protein: 7g; Sugar: 4g; Fiber: 7g

Equipment: Food processor; Serving bowl; Knife; Vegetable peeler.

Grilled Artichokes with Lemon Dip

Prep time: 15 min **Total time:** 35 min
Cook time: 20 min **Servings:** 4

Ingredients:

- ✓ 2 large artichokes
- ✓ 1 lemon, juiced (keep the zest for the dip)
- ✓ 2 tablespoons olive oil
- ✓ Salt and pepper, to taste
  For the Lemon Dip:
- ✓ 1/2 cup Greek yogurt or mayonnaise
- ✓ 1 garlic clove, minced
- ✓ Zest of 1 lemon
- ✓ 2 tablespoons fresh lemon juice
- ✓ 1 tablespoon fresh parsley, chopped
- ✓ Salt and pepper, to taste

Directions:

1. Preheat your grill to medium-high heat.
2. Cut the artichokes in half lengthwise. Use a spoon to remove the fuzzy center and any sharp leaves. Rinse them under cold water.
3. Bring a large pot of water to boil. Add the juice of one lemon to the water. Boil the artichoke halves for about 10 minutes to soften.
4. Drain the artichokes and let them cool for a few minutes.
5. Brush the artichokes with olive oil and season with salt and pepper.
6. Place the artichokes on the grill, cut side down. Grill for 5-7 minutes on each side or until they have nice grill marks.
7. While the artichokes are grilling, prepare the dip. In a bowl, mix together the Greek yogurt or mayonnaise, minced garlic, lemon zest, lemon juice, and chopped parsley. Season with salt and pepper to taste.
8. Serve the grilled artichokes warm with the lemon dip on the side.

Nutrition: Calories: 140; Fat: 8g; Carbs: 15g; Protein: 4g; Sugar: 2g; Fiber: 7g

Equipment: Grill; Large pot; Brush; Mixing bowl; Knife; Spoon.

Cucumber Rolls with Smoked Salmon and Cream Cheese

Prep time: 20 min
Cook time: 0 min
Total time: 20 min
Servings: 4

Ingredients:

- 1 large cucumber
- 4 ounces smoked salmon, thinly sliced
- 4 ounces cream cheese, softened
- 1 tablespoon fresh dill, finely chopped
- 1 teaspoon lemon zest
- 1 tablespoon lemon juice
- Salt and pepper to taste

Directions:

1. Using a vegetable peeler, slice the cucumber lengthwise into thin, wide ribbons.
2. In a mixing bowl, combine the cream cheese, dill, lemon zest, lemon juice, salt, and pepper. Mix until smooth.
3. Lay out a cucumber ribbon flat on a cutting board. Spread a thin layer of the cream cheese mixture over the entire surface.
4. Place a piece of smoked salmon on top, covering half of the cucumber slice.
5. Starting from the salmon side, carefully roll the cucumber slice, creating a tight roll.
6. Repeat with the remaining cucumber slices and filling.
7. Secure each roll with a toothpick if needed and arrange them on a serving plate.

Nutrition: Calories: 115; Fat: 8g; Carbs: 3g; Protein: 8g; Sugar: 2g; Fiber: 0.5g

Equipment: Vegetable peeler; Mixing bowl; Cutting board.

Zucchini and Parmesan Chips

Prep time: 15 min
Cook time: 20 min
Total time: 35 min
Servings: 4

Ingredients:

- 2 medium-sized zucchinis
- 1/2 cup grated Parmesan cheese
- 1/4 cup bread crumbs
- 1 teaspoon dried oregano
- 1/2 teaspoon garlic powder
- Salt and pepper to taste
- Olive oil spray

Directions:

1. Preheat the oven to 425°F (220°C) and line a baking sheet with parchment paper.
2. Slice the zucchinis into thin rounds, about 1/8-inch thick.
3. In a mixing bowl, combine the grated Parmesan, bread crumbs, dried oregano, garlic powder, salt, and pepper.
4. Dip each zucchini slice into the Parmesan mixture, ensuring both sides are coated, and place on the prepared baking sheet.
5. Lightly spray the coated zucchini slices with olive oil.
6. Bake in the preheated oven for 10 minutes. Flip the zucchini chips over and bake for an additional 10 minutes, or until they are golden brown and crispy.
7. Remove from the oven and let them cool slightly on the baking sheet before serving.

Nutrition: Calories: 85; Fat: 3.5g; Carbs: 7g; Protein: 6g; Sugar: 2g; Fiber: 1g

Equipment: Baking sheet; Mixing bowl; Knife; Parchment paper.

Baked Stuffed Figs with Walnuts and Feta

Prep time: 15 min **Total time:** 30 min
Cook time: 15 min **Servings:** 6

Ingredients:

- 12 fresh figs
- 1/2 cup walnuts, half chopped and half left as halves
- 1/3 cup feta cheese, crumbled
- 3 tablespoons honey
- 1/4 teaspoon ground cinnamon
- Zest of 1 orange
- Pinch of salt
- Fresh thyme sprigs, for garnish

Directions:

1. Preheat the oven to 350°F (175°C).
2. Carefully slice each fig in half lengthwise, without completely separating the two halves.
3. In a mixing bowl, combine the chopped walnuts, crumbled feta cheese, honey, cinnamon, orange zest, and a pinch of salt.
4. Gently stuff each fig half with the walnut and feta mixture, using a teaspoon or a small spatula.
5. Place the stuffed fig halves on a baking tray lined with parchment paper, with the stuffing facing up.
6. Place a walnut half on top of each stuffed fig for garnish.
7. Drizzle any remaining honey mixture over the stuffed figs.
8. Bake in the preheated oven for 10-15 minutes, or until the figs are soft and slightly caramelized.
9. Remove from the oven and immediately garnish each fig with a small sprig of fresh thyme.
10. Allow to cool for a few minutes before serving.

Nutrition: Calories: 140; Fat: 7g; Carbs: 19g; Protein: 4g; Sugar: 17g; Fiber: 2g

Equipment: Mixing bowl; Teaspoon or small spatula; Baking tray; Parchment paper.

DESSERT RECIPES

Lemon Sorbet

Prep time: 15 min **Total time:** 4 h 15 min
Freezing time: 4-5 hours **Servings:** 4

Ingredients:

- 1 cup granulated sugar
- 2 cups water
- 1 tbsp lemon zest
- 1 cup fresh lemon juice (about 4-5 lemons)
- 1 tbsp vodka (optional, to improve texture)

Directions:

1. In a medium saucepan, combine the sugar and water. Heat over medium heat, stirring occasionally, until the sugar completely dissolves. This will create a simple syrup.
2. Once the sugar is dissolved, remove the saucepan from the heat and allow it to cool for about 10 minutes.
3. Add the lemon zest and lemon juice to the saucepan, stirring well to combine.
4. If using, add the vodka. This helps in preventing the sorbet from becoming too icy and keeps the texture smooth.
5. Transfer the mixture to a bowl, cover, and refrigerate for at least 1 hour or until it's completely chilled.
6. Once chilled, pour the mixture into an ice cream maker and churn according to the manufacturer's instructions.
7. Transfer the churned sorbet to a lidded container and freeze for at least 3 hours, or until solid.
8. Before serving, let the sorbet sit out for 5-10 minutes to soften slightly. Scoop into bowls and serve immediately.

Nutrition: Calories: 190; Fat: 0g; Carbs: 49g; Protein: 0g; Sugar: 45g; Fiber: 0g

Equipment: Medium saucepan, stirring spoon, bowl, ice cream maker, lidded container.

Dates Stuffed with Nuts

Prep time: 20 min **Total time:** 20 min
Cook time: 0 min **Servings:** 4-6

Ingredients:

- 20 fresh Medjool dates
- 20 mixed nuts (e.g., almonds, walnuts, pecans, pistachios)
- Optional: A pinch of sea salt or fleur de sel to sprinkle

Directions:

1. Carefully slit each date lengthwise to remove the pit, ensuring not to cut the date in half completely.
2. Insert one nut into the center of each pitted date.
3. If desired, sprinkle a tiny pinch of sea salt or fleur de sel on top of each stuffed date. This will enhance the natural sweetness of the date and add a crunchy texture contrast.
4. Arrange the stuffed dates on a serving platter and serve immediately.

Nutrition: Calories: 65; Fat: 1g; Carbs: 15g; Protein: 1g; Sugar: 14g; Fiber: 2g

Equipment: Knife, serving platter.

Rice Pudding with Rose Water

Prep time: 10 min **Total time:** 55 min
Cook time: 45 min **Servings:** 4-6

Ingredients:

- 1 cup Arborio rice or short-grain rice
- 4 cups whole milk
- 1/2 cup granulated sugar
- 1 teaspoon vanilla extract
- 2 tablespoons rose water
- 1/4 teaspoon salt
- Optional garnish: rose petals, chopped pistachios, or almonds

Directions:

1. Rinse the rice under cold water until the water runs clear.
2. In a large saucepan, combine the rinsed rice, milk, and salt. Bring the mixture to a boil over medium-high heat.
3. Once boiling, reduce the heat to low and let it simmer. Stir occasionally to prevent sticking and burning.
4. When the rice is tender and the mixture starts to thicken (about 30 minutes), add the sugar and stir until dissolved.
5. Continue to cook for an additional 10-15 minutes, or until the mixture reaches a creamy consistency.
6. Remove the saucepan from heat and stir in the vanilla extract and rose water.
7. Transfer the rice pudding into serving dishes. Allow them to cool at room temperature for a bit before refrigerating.
8. Chill the rice pudding in the refrigerator for at least 2 hours before serving.
9. Before serving, garnish with rose petals, chopped pistachios, or almonds if desired.

Nutrition: Calories: 270; Fat: 4g; Carbs: 52g; Protein: 7g; Sugar: 28g; Fiber: 0g

Equipment: Large saucepan, measuring cups and spoons, stirring spoon, serving dishes.

Almond and Orange Blossom Cake

Prep time: 20 min **Total time:** 1 hour
Cook time: 40 min **Servings:** 8-10

Ingredients:

- 1 1/2 cups almond flour
- 1/2 cup all-purpose flour
- 1 1/2 teaspoons baking powder
- 1/4 teaspoon salt
- 3/4 cup granulated sugar
- 3 large eggs
- 1/2 cup unsalted butter, melted
- Zest of 1 orange
- 2 tablespoons orange blossom water

- ✓ Powdered sugar for dusting (optional)
- ✓ Sliced almonds for garnish (optional)

Nutrition: Calories: 290; Fat: 19g; Carbs: 25g; Protein: 6g; Sugar: 15g; Fiber: 2g

Equipment: Medium bowl, large bowl, whisk, 9-inch round cake pan, wire rack.

Chocolate Mousse with Olive Oil

Prep time: 20 min **Total time:** 2 h 20 min
Chilling time: 2 hours **Servings:** 4-6

Directions:

1. Preheat the oven to 350°F (175°C). Grease a 9-inch round cake pan or line it with parchment paper.
2. In a medium bowl, whisk together almond flour, all-purpose flour, baking powder, and salt. Set aside.
3. In a separate large bowl, beat the granulated sugar and eggs together until pale and frothy, about 3-4 minutes.
4. Slowly whisk in the melted butter until fully incorporated.
5. Gently fold in the dry ingredients just until combined.
6. Stir in the orange zest and orange blossom water.
7. Pour the batter into the prepared cake pan and smooth the top.
8. If desired, sprinkle the top with sliced almonds.
9. Bake in the preheated oven for 35-40 minutes, or until a toothpick inserted into the center comes out clean.
10. Remove from oven and allow the cake to cool in the pan for 10 minutes before transferring to a wire rack to cool completely.
11. Once cooled, dust the top with powdered sugar if desired before serving.

Ingredients:

- ✓ 200g dark chocolate (70% cocoa or higher), roughly chopped
- ✓ 3 large eggs, separated
- ✓ 1/4 cup high-quality extra virgin olive oil
- ✓ A pinch of sea salt
- ✓ 3 tablespoons granulated sugar
- ✓ Optional garnish: orange zest, flaky sea salt

Directions:

1. In a heatproof bowl, melt the dark chocolate over a pot of simmering water (double boiler method) until smooth. Remove from heat and allow it to cool slightly.
2. While the chocolate is cooling, whisk the egg yolks in a separate bowl until they are slightly thickened.

3. Gradually pour the olive oil into the yolks, whisking constantly until the mixture is smooth and emulsified.
4. Once the chocolate has cooled slightly, stir it into the egg yolk and olive oil mixture until smooth.
5. In a clean, dry bowl, whisk the egg whites with a pinch of sea salt until soft peaks form. Gradually add the sugar and continue whisking until stiff peaks form.
6. Gently fold the whipped egg whites into the chocolate mixture in two additions, ensuring the mixture remains light and airy.
7. Spoon the mousse into serving dishes and refrigerate for at least 2 hours, or until set.
8. Before serving, garnish with a sprinkle of orange zest and flaky sea salt if desired.

Nutrition: Calories: 310; Fat: 21g; Carbs: 25g; Protein: 5g; Sugar: 20g; Fiber: 2g

Equipment: Heatproof bowl, saucepan, two mixing bowls, whisk, spatula, serving dishes.

Fig Tartlets

Prep time: 30 min **Total time:** 50 min
Cook time: 20 min **Servings:** 6

Ingredients:

- 1 sheet of pre-made shortcrust pastry (or homemade if preferred)
- 12 fresh figs, halved
- 1/4 cup honey
- 1 teaspoon vanilla extract
- 1/2 cup mascarpone cheese or cream cheese
- Zest of 1 lemon
- Powdered sugar, for dusting (optional)
- Fresh mint leaves, for garnish (optional)

Directions:

1. Preheat the oven to 190°C (375°F).
2. Roll out the shortcrust pastry on a floured surface to a thickness of about 3mm. Using a cookie or pastry cutter, cut out 6 circles that will fit into your tartlet pans.
3. Press the pastry circles into the tartlet pans, ensuring they are snug against the sides. Trim any excess pastry using a knife.
4. Prick the base of each pastry with a fork multiple times to prevent it from puffing up during baking.
5. Bake the tartlet bases in the preheated oven for 10-12 minutes or until they are lightly golden. Remove from the oven and allow them to cool.
6. While the tartlet bases are cooling, mix the mascarpone cheese (or cream cheese), honey, vanilla extract, and lemon zest in a bowl until smooth.
7. Once the tartlet bases have cooled, spread a generous amount of the mascarpone mixture onto each base.
8. Arrange the halved figs on top of the mascarpone mixture, pressing them slightly into the mixture.
9. Drizzle a little honey over the figs, if desired.
10. Place the tartlets back into the oven and bake for an additional 8-10 minutes, or until the figs are slightly caramelized.
11. Allow the tartlets to cool slightly before serving. Dust with powdered sugar and garnish with fresh mint leaves if desired.

Nutrition: Calories: 290; Fat: 13g; Carbs: 40g; Protein: 4g; Sugar: 25g; Fiber: 3g

Equipment: Rolling pin, tartlet pans, bowl, whisk or spoon, knife, cookie or pastry cutter.

56-DAY MEAL PLAN

DAY	BREAKFAST	LUNCH	DINNER	SNACKS/DESSERTS	CALORIES (kcal)
1	Avocado and Tomato Whole Grain Toast (12)	Tomato and Mozzarella Caprese (24)	Grilled Salmon with Lemon Herb Butter (30)	Dates Stuffed with Nuts (65)	1015
2	Classic Greek Yogurt Parfait (11)	Grilled Chicken with Lemon and Thyme (40)	Sautéed Spinach with Garlic and Lemon (57)	Tomato and Mozzarella Skewers with Basil (60)	740
3	Scrambled Eggs with Spinach and Feta (11)	Cucumber and Radish Salad with Mint-Yogurt Dressing (22)	Pan-Seared Tuna Steaks with Capers (32)	Greek Tzatziki Sauce with Whole Grain Pita (60)	830
4	Fresh Fruit Smoothie Bowl with Chopped Nuts (17)	Broccoli and Feta Sauté (57)	Grilled Beef Kebabs with Tzatziki (43)	Cucumber Rolls with Smoked Salmon and Cream Cheese (63)	860
5	Mediterranean Omelet with Olives and Tomatoes (12)	Grilled Portobello Mushrooms with Garlic (55)	Grilled Sardines with Olive Tapenade (35)	Lemon Sorbet (65)	830
6	Almond Granola Parfait with Apricots (15)	Turkey Meatballs with Tomato Sauce (40)	Lentil Salad with Tomatoes and Cucumber (21)	Stuffed Olives with Feta Cheese (61)	950
7	Roasted Red Pepper and Feta Egg Muffins (19)	Lemon and Herb Grilled Swordfish (39)	Spinach and Strawberry Salad with Balsamic Vinaigrette (22)	Rice Pudding with Rose Water (66)	870
8	Chia Seed Pudding with Fresh Berries (13)	Zucchini Noodles with Pesto and Pine Nuts (52)	Baked Chicken with Olives and Capers (42)	Chocolate Mousse with Olive Oil (67)	1130
9	Veggie Frittata with Herbs (14)	Beet and Arugula Salad with Goat Cheese (25)	Baked Cod with Olives and Tomatoes (30)	Zucchini and Parmesan Chips (63)	835
10	Whole Grain Pancakes with Fig Compote (13)	Pork Chops Roasted Fennel and Tomatoes (43)	Greek Salad with Feta and Olives (20)	Hummus with Vegetable Sticks (61)	1115
11	Mediterranean Breakfast Salad with Prosciutto and Figs (15)	Roasted Trout with Almonds and Parsley (35)	Mediterranean Spaghetti Squash with Feta (53)	Fig Tartlets (68)	1150
12	Poached Eggs over Olive and Herb Focaccia (16)	Baked Artichokes with Lemon and Thyme (55)	Mediterranean Couscous Salad (26)	Almond and Orange Blossom Cake (66)	990

DAY	BREAKFAST	LUNCH	DINNER	SNACKS/DESSERTS	CALORIES (kcal)
13	Shakshuka with Bell Peppers and Tomatoes (17)	Lemon and Garlic Roast Chicken (46)	Pan-Seared Duck Breasts with Cherry Sauce (48)	Grilled Artichokes with Lemon Dip (62)	1190
14	Nut Butter and Banana Whole Grain Crepes (18)	Shrimp and Garlic Linguine (31)	Mussels in Tomato and Garlic Sauce (34)	Baked Stuffed Figs with Walnuts and Feta (64)	1210
15	Avocado and Tomato Whole Grain Toast (12)	Baked Eggplant with Tomato and Mozzarella (51)	Roasted Asparagus with Parmesan (56)	Dates Stuffed with Nuts (65)	805
16	Classic Greek Yogurt Parfait (11)	Marinated Zucchini Ribbon Salad with Pine Nuts (29)	Mediterranean Meatloaf with Sun-Dried Tomatoes (49)	Tomato and Mozzarella Skewers with Basil (60)	1015
17	Scrambled Eggs with Spinach and Feta (11)	Stuffed Chicken Breasts with Spinach and Feta (44)	Tuna and White Bean Salad (20)	Greek Tzatziki Sauce with Whole Grain Pita (60)	1105
18	Fresh Fruit Smoothie Bowl with Chopped Nuts (17)	Baked Halibut with Fennel, Cherry Tomatoes, and Olives (38)	Ratatouille with Fresh Basil (51)	Cucumber Rolls with Smoked Salmon and Cream Cheese (63)	785
19	Mediterranean Omelet with Olives and Tomatoes (12)	Quinoa and Roasted Vegetable Salad (23)	Kale and Pomegranate Salad (27)	Lemon Sorbet (65)	1015
20	Almond Granola Parfait with Apricots (15)	Herb-Crusted Rack of Lamb (46)	Fish Stew with Saffron and White Wine (32)	Stuffed Olives with Feta Cheese (61)	1160
21	Roasted Red Pepper and Feta Egg Muffins (19)	Stuffed Calamari with Rice and Herbs (33)	Spicy Octopus Salad (37)	Rice Pudding with Rose Water (66)	890
22	Veggie Frittata with Herbs (14)	Stuffed Bell Peppers with Rice and Herbs (53)	Clams with Chorizo and White Wine (36)	Chocolate Mousse with Olive Oil (67)	1310
23	Chia Seed Pudding with Fresh Berries (13)	Orzo and Shrimp Salad with Lemon Dressing (24)	Slow-Roasted Pork Shoulder with Sage (48)	Zucchini and Parmesan Chips (63)	1110
24	Whole Grain Pancakes with Fig Compote (13)	Chicken and Chorizo Paella (50)	Mediterranean Stuffed Zucchini Boats (59)	Hummus with Vegetable Sticks (61)	1215
25	Mediterranean Breakfast Salad with Prosciutto and Figs (15)	Warm Potato Salad with Dill and Mustard (28)	Roasted Butternut Squash with Sage (54)	Fig Tartlets (68)	970
26	Poached Eggs over Olive and Herb Focaccia (16)	Chickpea and Vegetable Curry (58)	Roast Lamb with Rosemary and Garlic (41)	Grilled Artichokes with Lemon Dip (62)	1350

DAY	BREAKFAST	LUNCH	DINNER	SNACKS/DESSERTS	CALORIES (kcal)
27	Shakshuka with Bell Peppers and Tomatoes (17)	Roasted Cauliflower Salad with Tahini Dressing (28)	Beef and Eggplant Moussaka (47)	Almond and Orange Blossom Cake (66)	1250
28	Nut Butter and Banana Whole Grain Crepes (18)	Braised Rabbit with Red Wine and Herbs (45)	Shrimp and Artichoke Paella (37)	Baked Stuffed Figs with Walnuts and Feta (64)	1400
29	Avocado and Tomato Whole Grain Toast (12)	Tomato and Mozzarella Caprese (24)	Grilled Salmon with Lemon Herb Butter (30)	Dates Stuffed with Nuts (65)	1015
30	Classic Greek Yogurt Parfait (11)	Grilled Chicken with Lemon and Thyme (40)	Sautéed Spinach with Garlic and Lemon (57)	Tomato and Mozzarella Skewers with Basil (60)	740
31	Scrambled Eggs with Spinach and Feta (11)	Cucumber and Radish Salad with Mint-Yogurt Dressing (22)	Pan-Seared Tuna Steaks with Capers (32)	Greek Tzatziki Sauce with Whole Grain Pita (60)	830
32	Fresh Fruit Smoothie Bowl with Chopped Nuts (17)	Broccoli and Feta Sauté (57)	Grilled Beef Kebabs with Tzatziki (43)	Cucumber Rolls with Smoked Salmon and Cream Cheese (63)	860
33	Mediterranean Omelet with Olives and Tomatoes (12)	Grilled Portobello Mushrooms with Garlic (55)	Grilled Sardines with Olive Tapenade (35)	Lemon Sorbet (65)	830
34	Almond Granola Parfait with Apricots (15)	Turkey Meatballs with Tomato Sauce (40)	Lentil Salad with Tomatoes and Cucumber (21)	Stuffed Olives with Feta Cheese (61)	950
35	Roasted Red Pepper and Feta Egg Muffins (19)	Lemon and Herb Grilled Swordfish (39)	Spinach and Strawberry Salad with Balsamic Vinaigrette (22)	Rice Pudding with Rose Water (66)	870
36	Chia Seed Pudding with Fresh Berries (13)	Zucchini Noodles with Pesto and Pine Nuts (52)	Baked Chicken with Olives and Capers (42)	Chocolate Mousse with Olive Oil (67)	1130
37	Veggie Frittata with Herbs (14)	Beet and Arugula Salad with Goat Cheese (25)	Baked Cod with Olives and Tomatoes (30)	Zucchini and Parmesan Chips (63)	835
38	Whole Grain Pancakes with Fig Compote (13)	Pork Chops Roasted Fennel and Tomatoes (43)	Greek Salad with Feta and Olives (20)	Hummus with Vegetable Sticks (61)	1115
39	Mediterranean Breakfast Salad with Prosciutto and Figs (15)	Roasted Trout with Almonds and Parsley (35)	Mediterranean Spaghetti Squash with Feta (53)	Fig Tartlets (68)	1150

DAY	BREAKFAST	LUNCH	DINNER	SNACKS/DESSERTS	CALORIES (kcal)
40	Poached Eggs over Olive and Herb Focaccia (16)	Baked Artichokes with Lemon and Thyme (55)	Mediterranean Couscous Salad (26)	Almond and Orange Blossom Cake (66)	990
41	Shakshuka with Bell Peppers and Tomatoes (17)	Lemon and Garlic Roast Chicken (46)	Pan-Seared Duck Breasts with Cherry Sauce (48)	Grilled Artichokes with Lemon Dip (62)	1190
42	Nut Butter and Banana Whole Grain Crepes (18)	Shrimp and Garlic Linguine (31)	Mussels in Tomato and Garlic Sauce (34)	Baked Stuffed Figs with Walnuts and Feta (64)	1210
43	Avocado and Tomato Whole Grain Toast (12)	Baked Eggplant with Tomato and Mozzarella (51)	Roasted Asparagus with Parmesan (56)	Dates Stuffed with Nuts (65)	805
44	Classic Greek Yogurt Parfait (11)	Marinated Zucchini Ribbon Salad with Pine Nuts (29)	Mediterranean Meatloaf with Sun-Dried Tomatoes (49)	Tomato and Mozzarella Skewers with Basil (60)	1015
45	Scrambled Eggs with Spinach and Feta (11)	Stuffed Chicken Breasts with Spinach and Feta (44)	Tuna and White Bean Salad (20)	Greek Tzatziki Sauce with Whole Grain Pita (60)	1105
46	Fresh Fruit Smoothie Bowl with Chopped Nuts (17)	Baked Halibut with Fennel, Cherry Tomatoes, and Olives (38)	Ratatouille with Fresh Basil (51)	Cucumber Rolls with Smoked Salmon and Cream Cheese (63)	785
47	Mediterranean Omelet with Olives and Tomatoes (12)	Quinoa and Roasted Vegetable Salad (23)	Kale and Pomegranate Salad (27)	Lemon Sorbet (65)	1015
48	Almond Granola Parfait with Apricots (15)	Herb-Crusted Rack of Lamb (46)	Fish Stew with Saffron and White Wine (32)	Stuffed Olives with Feta Cheese (61)	1160
49	Roasted Red Pepper and Feta Egg Muffins (19)	Stuffed Calamari with Rice and Herbs (33)	Spicy Octopus Salad (37)	Rice Pudding with Rose Water (66)	890
50	Veggie Frittata with Herbs (14)	Stuffed Bell Peppers with Rice and Herbs (53)	Clams with Chorizo and White Wine (36)	Chocolate Mousse with Olive Oil (67)	1310
51	Chia Seed Pudding with Fresh Berries (13)	Orzo and Shrimp Salad with Lemon Dressing (24)	Slow-Roasted Pork Shoulder with Sage (48)	Zucchini and Parmesan Chips (63)	1110
52	Whole Grain Pancakes with Fig Compote (13)	Chicken and Chorizo Paella (50)	Mediterranean Stuffed Zucchini Boats (59)	Hummus with Vegetable Sticks (61)	1215
53	Mediterranean Breakfast Salad with Prosciutto and Figs (15)	Warm Potato Salad with Dill and Mustard (28)	Roasted Butternut Squash with Sage (54)	Fig Tartlets (68)	970

DAY	BREAKFAST	LUNCH	DINNER	SNACKS/ DESSERTS	CALORIES (kcal)
54	Poached Eggs over Olive and Herb Focaccia (16)	Chickpea and Vegetable Curry (58)	Roast Lamb with Rosemary and Garlic (41)	Grilled Artichokes with Lemon Dip (62)	1350
55	Shakshuka with Bell Peppers and Tomatoes (17)	Roasted Cauliflower Salad with Tahini Dressing (28)	Beef and Eggplant Moussaka (47)	Almond and Orange Blossom Cake (66)	1250
56	Nut Butter and Banana Whole Grain Crepes (18)	Braised Rabbit with Red Wine and Herbs (45)	Shrimp and Artichoke Paella (37)	Baked Stuffed Figs with Walnuts and Feta (64)	1400

COOKING CONVERSION CHART

Volume Equivalents (Dry)

US Standard	Metric (approximate)
1/8 teaspoon	0.5 mL
1/4 teaspoon	1 mL
1/2 teaspoon	2 mL
3/4 teaspoon	4 mL
1 teaspoon	5 mL
1 tablespoon	15 mL
1/4 cup	59 mL
1/3 cup	79 mL
1/2 cup	118 mL
2/3 cup	156 mL
3/4 cup	177 mL
1 cup	235 mL
2 cups or 1 pint	475 mL
3 cups	700 mL
4 cups or 1 quart	1 L

Volume Equivalents (Liquid)

US Standard	US Standard (ounces)	Metric (approximate)
2 tablespoons	1 fl. oz.	30 mL
1/4 cup	2 fl. oz.	60 mL
1/2 cup	4 fl. oz.	120 mL
1 cup	8 fl. oz.	240 mL
1 1/2 cup	12 fl. oz.	355 mL
2 cups or 1 pint	16 fl. oz.	475 mL
4 cups or 1 quart	32 fl. oz.	1 L
1 gallon	128 fl. oz.	4 L

Oven Temperatures

Fahrenheit (F)	Celsius (C) (approximate)
250	120
300	150
325	165
350	180
375	190
400	200
425	220
450	230

Weight Equivalents

US Standard	Metric (approximate)
1/2 ounce	15 g
1 ounce	30 g
2 ounces	60 g
4 ounces	115 g
8 ounces	225 g
12 ounces	340 g
16 ounces or 1 pound	455 g

SHOPPING LISTS WEEKS 1 AND 5 *

Ingredient	Quantity	Unit
Almonds, slivered	1	tablespoon
Anchovy Paste	1/2	teaspoon
Arborio Rice	1/2	cup
Balsamic Vinegar	2 1/3	tablespoons
Bananas	2	bananas
Beef Sirloin	250	grams
Black Olives (Kalamata)	1/2	cup
Black Pepper	1	teaspoon
Blueberries	1/2	cup
Boneless Chicken Breasts	2	pcs
Breadcrumbs	1/8	cup
Broccoli	2	cups
Capers	2	tablespoons
Cherry Tomatoes	1 1/2	cups
Chia Seeds	1	tablespoon
Cooking spray or butter	-	for greasing
Cream Cheese	2	ounces
Crushed Tomatoes	1/2	28 oz
Cucumber	4	medium
Dried Basil	1/2	teaspoon
Dried Oregano	1	teaspoon
Extra-Virgin Olive Oil	12	cups
Feta Cheese	1 1/2	cups
Fresh Apricots	4	pieces
Fresh Basil Leaves	1/3	cup
Fresh Dill	2	tablespoons
Fresh Medjool Dates	10	pcs
Fresh Mint Leaves	4	tablespoons
Fresh Mozzarella Cheese	1/2	pound
Fresh Parsley	10	tablespoons
Fresh Rosemary	1/2	tablespoon
Fresh Sardines	6	pcs
Fresh Spinach	11	cups
Fresh Thyme	1/2	tablespoon
Fresh Tuna Steaks	2	6-8 oz each
Garlic Cloves	17	cloves
Goat Cheese	1/8	cup
Granola	1	cup
Granulated Sugar	3/4	cup
Parmesan Cheese	1/8	cup
Greek Yogurt	5	cups
Green or Brown Lentils	1/2	cup
Ground Turkey	1/2	lb
Honey	7	tablespoons
Kiwi	1/2	cup
Large Eggs	15	pcs
Large Green Olives	8	pcs
Portobello Mushrooms	2	large
Lemon Juice	2	tablespoons
Lemon Thyme Sprigs	2	pcs
Lemon Zest	1	tablespoon
Lemons	9	pcs
Maple Syrup	1 1/2	tablespoons
Medium Cucumber	1/3	pc
Medium Tomato	1	pc
Milk	2	cups
Mini Mozzarella Balls	8	pcs
Mixed Berries	1	cup
Mixed Nuts	1/2	cup
Olives	1/4	cup
Onion	1	pc
Paprika	1/2	teaspoon
Radishes	4	pcs
Red Bell Pepper	1	pc
Red Chili Flakes	1/2	teaspoon
Red Onion	1/8	cup
Red Pepper Flakes	-	optional
Ripe Avocado	1	whole
Ripe Tomatoes	2	large
Roasted Red Pepper	1	pc
Roasted Walnuts	1/8	cup
Rose Water	1	tablespoon
Salmon Fillets	2	6-8 oz each
Salt	1/2	teaspoon
Sea Salt or Fleur de Sel	1/4	teaspoon
Shredded Coconut	A pinch	optional
Smoked Salmon	2	ounces
Strawberries	1 1/2	cups
Swordfish Steaks	2	6-8 oz each
Unsalted Butter	1/3	cup
Vanilla Extract	1 1/2	teaspoons
Vodka	1/2	tablespoon
Whole Almonds	1/8	cup
Whole Grain Bread	2	slices
Whole Grain Pita Breads	2	pieces

SHOPPING LISTS WEEKS 2 AND 6 *

Ingredient	Quantity	Unit
All-purpose Flour	1/4	cup
Almond Flour	1	cup
Arugula	2	cups
Baking Powder	2	teaspoons

Baking Soda	1/2	teaspoon
Balsamic Vinegar	3	tablespoons
Bell Peppers	2 1/4	cups
Black Olives	1/2	cup
Black Pepper	1/4	teaspoon
Bread Crumbs	1/4	cup
Buttermilk	1	cup
Canned Chickpeas	1	400 grams
Canned Diced Tomatoes	1	8 oz
Capers	1/4	cup
Carrot	1	pc
Cayenne Pepper	1/4	teaspoon
Celery Stalk	1	pc
Cherry Tomatoes	4	cups
Chia Seeds	1/4	cup
Chicken (Thighs or Breasts)	2	pieces
Chicken Broth	1/2	cup
Cinnamon	1/2	teaspoon
Cod Fillets	2	6-8 oz each
Diced Tomatoes	2	cups
Cucumbers	2	pcs
Cumin	1/2	teaspoon
Dark Chocolate (70% cocoa or higher)	100	grams
Dried Oregano	2	teaspoons
Dry White Wine	1/4	cup
Duck Breasts	1	200 grams
Extra-Virgin Olive Oil	2	cups
Feta Cheese	2	cups
Fresh Basil Leaves	1	cup
Fresh Berries	1/2	cup
Fresh Cherries	100	grams
Fresh Dill	1/4	cup
Fresh Figs	30	pcs
Fresh Herbs (parsley, chives, basil)	2	tablespoons
Fresh Mint Leaves	1/4	cup
Fresh Mussels	1	pound
Fresh Parsley	1	cup
Fresh Rosemary	1	sprig
Fresh Thyme	10	sprigs
Garlic Cloves	20	pcs
Garlic Powder	1/4	teaspoon
Goat Cheese	1/4	cup
Granulated Sugar	1/2	cup
Parmesan Cheese	1/4	cup
Greek Yogurt	1/4	cup
Green Bell Pepper	1	pc
Green Olives	1/4	cup
Green Onions (Scallions)	1/4	cup
Honey	1	cup
Kalamata Olives	1	cup
Large Artichokes	1	pc
Large Eggs	19	pcs
Large Fennel Bulbs	1	pc
Large Shrimp	1/2	pound
Lemon Juice	3	tablespoons
Lemons	8	pieces
Linguine Pasta	1/2	pound
Maple Syrup	3	tablespoons
Mascarpone or Cream Cheese	1/4	cup
Medium Onion	1	pc
Medium-sized Beets	2	pcs
Milk	1	cup
Mixed Greens	2	cups
Nut Butter	4	tablespoons
Olive and Herb Focaccia	2	slices
Paprika	1	teaspoon
Pine Nuts	1/3	cup
Pork Chops	2	6-8 oz each
Powdered Sugar	1	tablespoon
Prosciutto	4	slices
Red Pepper Flakes	1/2	teaspoon
Red Wine	1/4	cup
Red Wine Vinegar	1	tablespoon
Ripe Bananas	2	pcs
Ripe Tomatoes	2	large
Salt	1	teaspoon
Shallot	1	pc
Shortcrust Pastry Sheet	1	sheet
Sliced Almonds	1/3	cup
Spaghetti Squash	1/2	medium
Tahini	2	tablespoons
Trout Fillets	2	6-8 oz each
Unsalted Butter	1/2	cup
Unswt. Almond Milk	1	cup
Vanilla Extract	2	teaspoons
Walnuts	2/3	cup
White Vinegar	1	tablespoon
White Wine	1/4	cup
Whole Artichokes	2	pcs
Whole Chicken	1/3	4-5 lb
Whole Grain Couscous	1/2	cup
Whole Grain Flour	1 1/2	cups
Yellow Bell Pepper	1	pc
Yellow Onion	1	pc
Zucchini	2	pcs

SHOPPING LISTS WEEKS 3 AND 7 *

Ingredient	Quantity	Unit
Almond granola	1	cup
Almond milk	1	cup
Almonds, slivered	1	tablespoon
Balsamic vinegar	1	tablespoon
Bananas	2	pcs
Bay Leaf	1	pc
Black olives	1/4	cup
Black pepper	1	teaspoon
Blueberries	1/2	cup
Breadcrumbs	1/2	cup
Carrot	1	pc
Cherry Tomatoes	3	cups
Chia seeds	1	tablespoon
Chicken Breasts	2	pcs
Chicken or Vegetable Broth	1/2	cup
Cilantro Leaves	1	handful
Cooking spray or butter	-	for greasing
Cream cheese	2	ounces
Cucumber	3	medium
Dijon Mustard	1	tablespoon
Dried Oregano	2	teaspoons
Dried Rosemary	1/4	teaspoon
Dried Thyme	1/2	teaspoon
Dry White Wine	1/4	cup
Eggplants	2	medium
Eggs	15	large
Extra-Virgin Olive Oil	1 1/3	cups
Fennel Bulb	1	pc
Feta Cheese	2 1/2	cups
Fish Fillets	2	pcs
Fish or Vegetable Broth	1	cup
Fresh apricots	4	pcs
Fresh Asparagus	250	grams
Fresh Basil	13	leaves
Fresh Breadcrumbs	1/2	cup
Fresh Dill	1/4	cup
Fresh lemon juice	1 1/2	tablespoons
Fresh Medjool Dates	10	pcs
Fresh Mint	1/8	cup
Fresh Octopus	250	grams
Fresh Parsley	1	cup
Fresh Rosemary	1	tablespoon
Fresh Spinach	5 1/2	cups
Fresh Thyme	1	tablespoon
Garlic Cloves	15	cloves
Goat cheese	1/8	cup
Granulated Sugar	3/4	cup
Greek yogurt	4	cups
Green Bell Pepper	1/2	pc
Green Olives	1/4	cup
Green onions	1/8	cup
Ground Beef	170	grams
Ground Lamb	170	grams
Halibut Fillets	2	6-8 oz each
Honey	9	tablespoons
Kalamata Olives	1/2	cup
Kale	2	cups
Kiwi	1/2	cup
Large Calamari Tubes	4	pcs
Green olives (pitted)	12	large
Lemon zest	1	teaspoon
Lemons	7	pcs
Limes	1	pc
Maple Syrup	2	teaspoons
Milk	3	cups
Mini mozzarella balls (bocconcini)	8	pcs
Mint leaves	3	leaves
Mixed berries	1	cup
Mixed Nuts	1/2	cup
Mozzarella Cheese	100	grams
Onion	2	pcs
Parmesan Cheese	1/2	cup
Pea shoot microgreens	-	for garnish
Pine nuts	1/8	cup
Pomegranate	1	pc
Quinoa	1/2	cup
Racks of Lamb	1	7-8 ribs/pc
Red Bell Pepper	2	pcs
Red chili flakes	1	teaspoon
Red Chili Peppers	1	pc
Red Onion	3	pcs
Rice Vinegar	1/2	tablespoon
Ripe avocado	1	pc
Roasted red pepper	1	pc
Rose Petals, Pistachios, Almonds	-	for garnish
Rose Water	1	tablespoon
Saffron Threads	-	A pinch

Ingredient	Quantity	Unit
Salt	1/2	teaspoon
Short-Grain Rice	1/2	cup
Shredded coconut	-	A pinch
Smoked salmon	2	ounces
Spring Onions	1	pc
Strawberries	1/2	cup
Sun-Dried Tomatoes	1/4	cup
Tomatoes	5	medium
Tuna in olive oil (canned)	1/2	5 oz
Uncooked Rice	1/2	cup
Vanilla Extract	1 1/2	teaspoons
Vodka	1/2	tablespoon
Walnuts	1/4	cup
White beans (canned)	1/2	14 oz
Whole grain bread	4	slices
Yellow Bell Pepper	1	pc
Zucchinis	3	medium

SHOPPING LISTS WEEKS 4 AND 8 *

Ingredient	Quantity	Unit
All-purpose Flour	1/3	cup
Almond Flour	1/2	cup
Unswt. Almond Milk	1	cup
Apple cider vinegar	1	tablespoon
Arborio or Paella Rice	1	cup
Artichoke Hearts (canned/jarred)	1/2	cup
Artichokes	1	large
Baking Powder	1	teaspoon
Baking soda	1/4	teaspoon
Balsamic vinegar	1	tablespoon
Bay Leaves	1	pc
Beef or Chicken Broth	1/2	cup
Bell Peppers (red and yellow)	8	large
Black Pepper	1/4	teaspoon
Bone-in Leg of Lamb	2	lbs
Bread crumbs	1/4	cup
Broth	5	cups
Brown Rice	1/2	cup
Butter	1/4	cup
Buttermilk	1/2	cup
Butternut Squash	1	medium
Carrots	3	medium
Cauliflower	1	medium
Cayenne pepper	1/2	teaspoon

Ingredient	Quantity	Unit
Celery Stalk	1	pc
Cherry Tomatoes	2	cups
Chia seeds	1/4	cup
Chicken Thighs	150	grams
Chickpeas	2	cans
Chili Powder	1/4	teaspoon
Chorizo Sausage	200	grams
Cinnamon	1/2	teaspoon
Coconut Milk	1	cup
Cooked Quinoa	1/2	cup
Crumbled feta cheese	-	for garnish
Crusty Bread	-	for serving
Cucumbers	1	medium
Cumin	1/2	teaspoon
Curry Powder	1	tablespoon
Dark Chocolate (70% cocoa or higher)	100	grams
Dried Oregano	1	teaspoon
Eggplants	1	large
Eggs	20	large
Extra-Virgin Olive Oil	1 1/2	cups
Feta Cheese	1	cup
Fresh Basil	1/4	cup
Fresh berries	1/2	cup
Fresh Clams	1	lbs
Fresh dill	1/4	cup
Fresh Figs	20	pcs
Fresh herbs (parsley, chives, basil)	2	tablespoons
Fresh Mint	2	tablespoons
Fresh Parsley	1 1/2	cups
Fresh Rosemary	3	sprigs
Fresh Sage Leaves	12	pcs
Fresh Thyme	5	sprigs
Frozen Peas	1/2	cup
Garlic	20	cloves
Garlic powder	1/4	teaspoon
Ginger	1/2	tablespoon
Granulated Sugar	1/3	cup
Parmesan Cheese	2/3	cup
Greek yogurt	1/4	cup
Green Beans	100	grams
Green onions (scallions)	1/4	cup
Ground Beef	200	grams
Ground Cinnamon	1/2	teaspoon
Ground Cumin	1	teaspoon
Ground Turmeric	1/2	teaspoon
Honey	1/2	cup
Kalamata olives	1/4	cup
Large Shrimp	1	pound

Lemon	3	pcs
Lemon juice	2	tablespoons
Lime	1	pc
Maple Syrup	2	tablespoons
Mascarpone or Cream Cheese	1/4	cup
Milk	2	cups
Mixed greens	2	cups
Mozzarella Cheese	100	grams
Nut butter	4	tablespoons
Olive and herb focaccia	2	slices
Onions	6	large
Orange (for zest)	1	pc
Orange Blossom Water	1/2	tablespoon
Orange Zest, Flaky Sea Salt	-	for garnish
Orzo pasta	1/2	cup
Paprika	1	teaspoon
Pomegranate seeds	1/8	cup
Pork Shoulder (bone-in)	2	lbs
Prosciutto	4	slices
Rabbit	1/2	whole
Red Chili Flakes	-	for sprinkle
Red Onion	1/2	cup
Red Pepper Flakes	1/4	teaspoon
Red Wine	1 1/2	cups
Ripe bananas	2	pcs
Saffron Threads	1/2	teaspoon
Salt	to taste	
Sea Salt	1/4	teaspoon
Shortcrust Pastry Sheet	1/2	pc
Sliced Almonds	-	for garnish
Small Potatoes	1	lbs
Smoked Paprika	1/2	teaspoon
Spinach	100	grams
Tahini	1/4	cup
Tomato Paste	1	tablespoon
Tomatoes	5	pcs
Vanilla Extract	1 1/2	teaspoons
Walnuts	1/4	cup
White vinegar	1	tablespoon
White Wine	1/4	cup
Whole grain flour	1	cup
Whole grain mustard	1	tablespoon
Zucchinis	4	medium

* Understanding Your Mediterranean Diet Weekly Shopping List

- **Servings:** The quantities listed are calculated for two servings. So, if you're cooking for one, simply halve the quantities. For more servings, multiply accordingly.
- **Optional Items:** Ingredients marked as "optional," "to taste," or "as desired" in recipes may not be included in this list. Feel free to add them as you wish.
- **Rounded Measurements:** The quantities may be rounded up or down to match standard units. For example, if a recipe calls for a third of a cup, it's rounded to the nearest standard measurement for your convenience.
- **Substitutions:** If you have dietary restrictions or just don't like certain items, feel free to swap them out. For instance, almond milk can often be exchanged for dairy milk.
- **Storage:** Be aware of perishable items and consider storage. For example, fresh herbs can spoil quickly, so you may want to opt for dried versions if you don't plan to use them right away.
- **Local Availability:** Some Mediterranean ingredients might not be as readily available in all U.S. locations. Look for substitutes that maintain the spirit of the Mediterranean diet—think fresh, unprocessed, and colorful.

Keep this list handy when you go shopping, and feel free to tweak it to match your personal preferences and needs. Happy cooking!

INDEX

- Almond and Orange Blossom Cake (**66**)
- Almond Granola Parfait with Apricots (**15**)
- Avocado and Tomato Whole Grain Toast (**12**)
- Baked Artichokes with Lemon and Thyme (**55**)
- Baked Chicken with Olives and Capers (**42**)
- Baked Cod with Olives and Tomatoes (**30**)
- Baked Eggplant with Tomato and Mozzarella (**51**)
- Baked Halibut with Fennel, Cherry Tomatoes, and Olives (**38**)
- Baked Stuffed Figs with Walnuts and Feta (**64**)
- Beef and Eggplant Moussaka (**47**)
- Beet and Arugula Salad with Goat Cheese (**25**)
- Braised Rabbit with Red Wine and Herbs (**45**)
- Broccoli and Feta Sauté (**57**)
- Chia Seed Pudding with Fresh Berries (**13**)
- Chicken and Chorizo Paella (**50**)
- Chickpea and Vegetable Curry (**58**)
- Chocolate Mousse with Olive Oil (**67**)
- Clams with Chorizo and White Wine (**36**)
- Classic Greek Yogurt Parfait (**11**)
- Cucumber and Radish Salad with Mint-Yogurt Dressing (**22**)
- Cucumber Rolls with Smoked Salmon and Cream Cheese (**63**)
- Dates Stuffed with Nuts (**65**)
- Fig Tartlets (**68**)
- Fish Stew with Saffron and White Wine (**32**)
- Fresh Fruit Smoothie Bowl with Chopped Nuts (**17**)
- Greek Salad with Feta and Olives (**20**)
- Greek Tzatziki Sauce with Whole Grain Pita (**60**)
- Grilled Artichokes with Lemon Dip (**62**)
- Grilled Beef Kebabs with Tzatziki (**43**)
- Grilled Chicken with Lemon and Thyme (**40**)
- Grilled Eggplant and Bell Pepper Salad (**26**)
- Grilled Portobello Mushrooms with Garlic (**55**)
- Grilled Salmon with Lemon Herb Butter (**30**)
- Grilled Sardines with Olive Tapenade (**35**)
- Herb-Crusted Rack of Lamb (**46**)
- Hummus with Vegetable Sticks (**61**)
- Kale and Pomegranate Salad (**27**)
- Lemon and Garlic Roast Chicken (**46**)
- Lemon and Herb Grilled Swordfish (**39**)
- Lemon Sorbet (**65**)
- Lentil Salad with Tomatoes and Cucumber (**21**)
- Marinated Zucchini Ribbon Salad with Pine Nuts (**29**)
- Mediterranean Breakfast Salad with Prosciutto and Figs (**15**)
- Mediterranean Couscous Salad (**26**)
- Mediterranean Meatloaf with Sun-Dried Tomatoes (**49**)
- Mediterranean Omelet with Olives and Tomatoes (**12**)
- Mediterranean Spaghetti Squash with Feta (**53**)
- Mediterranean Stuffed Zucchini Boats (**59**)
- Mussels in Tomato and Garlic Sauce (**34**)
- Nut Butter and Banana Whole Grain Crepes (**18**)
- Orzo and Shrimp Salad with Lemon Dressing (**24**)
- Pan-Seared Duck Breasts with Cherry Sauce (**48**)
- Pan-Seared Tuna Steaks with Capers (**32**)
- Poached Eggs over Olive and Herb Focaccia (**16**)
- Pork Chops Roasted Fennel and Tomatoes (**43**)
- Quinoa and Roasted Vegetable Salad (**23**)
- Ratatouille with Fresh Basil (**51**)
- Rice Pudding with Rose Water (**66**)
- Roast Lamb with Rosemary and Garlic (**41**)
- Roasted Asparagus with Parmesan (**56**)
- Roasted Butternut Squash with Sage (**54**)
- Roasted Cauliflower Salad with Tahini Dressing (**28**)
- Roasted Red Pepper and Feta Egg Muffins (**19**)
- Roasted Trout with Almonds and Parsley (**35**)
- Sautéed Spinach with Garlic and Lemon (**57**)
- Scrambled Eggs with Spinach and Feta (**11**)
- Shakshuka with Bell Peppers and Tomatoes (**17**)
- Shrimp and Artichoke Paella (**37**)
- Shrimp and Garlic Linguine (**31**)
- Slow-Roasted Pork Shoulder with Sage (**48**)
- Spicy Octopus Salad (**37**)
- Spinach and Strawberry Salad with Balsamic Vinaigrette (**22**)
- Stuffed Bell Peppers with Rice and Herbs (**53**)
- Stuffed Calamari with Rice and Herbs (**33**)
- Stuffed Chicken Breasts with Spinach and Feta (**44**)
- Stuffed Olives with Feta Cheese (**61**)
- Tomato and Mozzarella Caprese (**24**)
- Tomato and Mozzarella Skewers with Basil (**60**)
- Tuna and White Bean Salad (**20**)
- Turkey Meatballs with Tomato Sauce (**40**)
- Veggie Frittata with Herbs (**14**)
- Warm Potato Salad with Dill and Mustard (**28**)
- Whole Grain Pancakes with Fig Compote (**13**)
- Zucchini and Parmesan Chips (**63**)
- Zucchini Noodles with Pesto and Pine Nuts (**52**)

Conclusion

As the last pages of our exploration are gently turned, the music of the Mediterranean lifestyle resonates still. The journey was not merely across miles, but through years of culture, lives intertwined with nature, and a gastronomic adventure that has stood the testament of time. The echoes of the Mediterranean, you'll find, remain long after the final notes have been played.

This journey was not about sprinting to a destination; it was about slowing down to savor each note, each chord, each rhythm. The Mediterranean lifestyle is about balance and harmony, about finding joy in simple pleasures, about making peace with oneself and the world.

As the final note in our symphony lingers, may you carry this melody in your heart, and may it become the soundtrack to your life. Adopt the principles of the Mediterranean lifestyle, let them shape your days, guide your choices, and color your world.

So here's to the melody of the Mediterranean, a melody as timeless as the sea, as enduring as the mountains, as vibrant as the marketplaces. May its song be your guide, its rhythm your dance, its harmony your peace. And may the Mediterranean symphony play on, through the seasons of your life, echoing the celebration of health, happiness, and heartiness.

As we conclude this voyage, remember dear reader, every end is but the beginning of a new journey. And so, the symphony plays on, resonating in the silence, echoing in the whispers of the wind, the rustling of the leaves, the rolling of the waves. Let it guide you, let it inspire you, let it be the music to which you dance, not just today, not just tomorrow, but always.

Here's to you, dear reader, for journeying with us, for dancing to our tune, for being a part of our symphony. May the rhythm stay with you, the melody inspires you, and the music never stops. For the symphony of life plays on, and so shall we.

Copyright © 2024 by Vita Nourish

All rights reserved. No part of this book may be reproduced, distributed, or transmitted in any form or by any means, including photocopying, recording, or other electronic or mechanical methods, without the prior written permission of the publisher, except in the case of brief quotations embodied in critical reviews and certain other noncommercial uses permitted by copyright law.

Legal Notice. The information contained in this book is intended for educational and informational purposes only and is not a substitute for professional medical advice or treatment. Consult with a qualified healthcare professional before making any changes to your diet or lifestyle. The author and publisher expressly disclaim responsibility for any adverse effects that may result from the use or application of the information contained in this book.

Disclaimer. While every effort has been made to ensure the accuracy and reliability of the information contained in this book, neither the author nor the publisher can assume responsibility for errors, inaccuracies, or omissions. The reader is advised to consult with healthcare providers for specific health-related issues and should exercise caution when preparing recipes, particularly for allergies and dietary restrictions.

FREE BONUS

Dear Friend,

Thank you for choosing "The Complete Mediterranean Diet Cookbook for Beginners" as your trusted companion on this remarkable journey to better health and wellness. By embracing the Mediterranean diet, you're not merely adopting a set of eating habits; you're participating in an age-old tradition that offers unparalleled benefits for both mind and body. A diet rich in colorful fruits, nutritious vegetables, and heart-healthy fats not only pleases the palate but also fortifies your health, backed by science's unwavering support.

To claim your **70+ BONUS PDF RECIPES**, please send an email to **the.nutrabook@gmail.com** with your Amazon order number. We will promptly respond with your bonus recipes. We are committed to enhancing your culinary experiences and well-being with each edition of our books. Your satisfaction drives us to improve, innovate, and fine-tune the resources we provide. We highly value your thoughts, suggestions, and constructive criticisms, so please don't hesitate to share them with us at the same email address. Your feedback is not just welcome; it's essential.

As you continue your voyage through the world of healthful eating, know that this book is but one star in a constellation of resources we offer. Our series of Mediterranean diet books and other dietary and culinary adventures can be accessed through the author's page **amazon.com/stores/author/B0CGX7D4M9**.

Now, we kindly ask for a small favor. As a small, independent publisher, each review carries a great deal of significance for us. Your thoughts not only inspire us to keep improving but also help prospective readers make informed choices. If you found both this book and the bonus recipes valuable and enlightening, would you please take a moment to share your thoughts by leaving a review on Amazon? Your insights can significantly help others seeking the path to healthier living, just as you are. You'll find the link and a QR code below for your convenience.

Your opinion is a beacon for others in their journey toward health, and we greatly appreciate you for illuminating the path.

Thank you for allowing us to be a part of your transformative culinary adventure. We wish you continued health and endless enjoyment through the wonders of the Mediterranean lifestyle.

With heartfelt gratitude,

Nutra Book Team

Made in the USA
Las Vegas, NV
27 November 2023